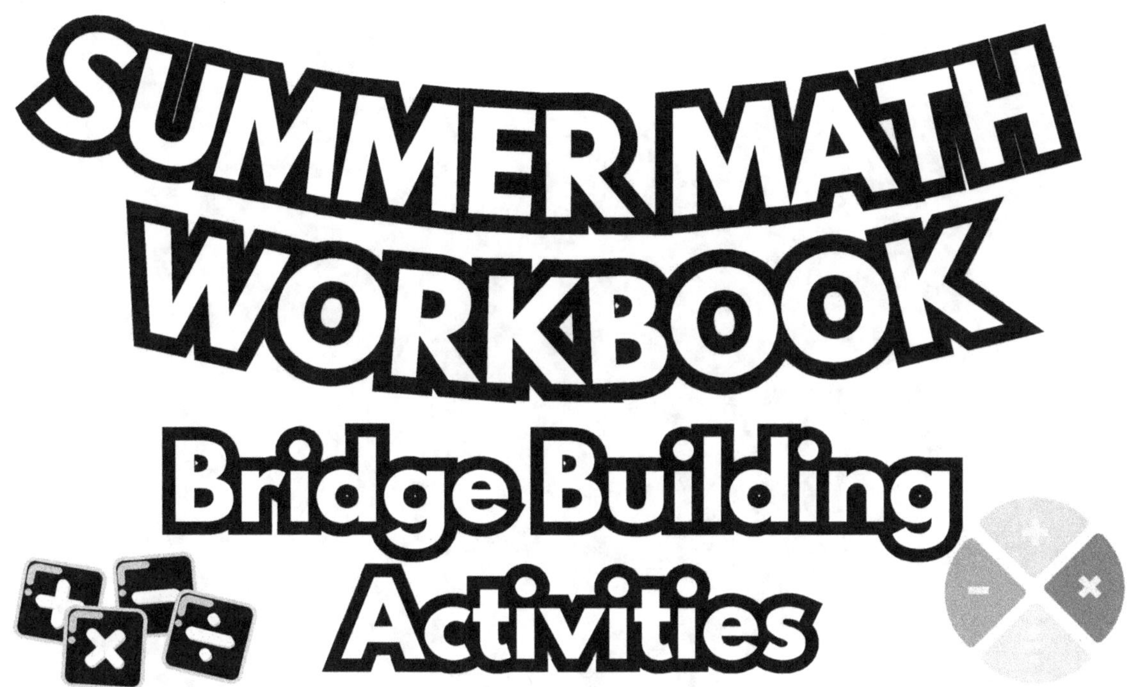

SUMMER MATH WORKBOOK
Bridge Building Activities

Copyright © 2024-25 Summer Bridge Building Activities.
All rights reserved. This book or any portion thereof may not be reproduced or used in any manner whatsoever without the express written permission of the publisher except for the use of brief quotations in a book review.

Introduction

As parents and educators, we understand the pivotal role that mathematics plays in shaping a child's academic journey and future success. Yet, the path to mathematical proficiency can often seem daunting, filled with challenges and complexities. That's where the transformative power of Summer Bridge Building Activities books comes into play, illuminating the way forward with clarity, precision, and purpose.

Summer vacation is a time for rest and relaxation, but it also presents the risk of the "summer slide," where students lose some of the academic gains they made during the school year. Summer Bridge Building Activities books are specifically designed to tackle this challenge, ensuring that your child stays academically engaged and prepared for the upcoming school year. These books provide a seamless bridge from one grade to the next, reinforcing essential skills and introducing new concepts that will give your child a head start.

Imagine your child eagerly diving into the pages of a Summer Bridge Building Activities book, greeted by clear, engaging content that demystifies complex mathematical concepts. With each turn of the pages, they embark on a journey of discovery, encountering thoughtfully curated practice questions that reinforce learning and sharpen problem-solving skills. As they unveil the answers to those questions, a sense of accomplishment blossoms within them — a tangible reward for their hard work and dedication.

Summer Bridge Building Activities books transcend traditional educational tools; they are meticulously crafted to build a deep and enduring understanding of mathematics. These books follow a sequential and logical progression, starting from fundamental principles and advancing to sophisticated problem-solving strategies. Each chapter is designed to build on the previous one, ensuring a solid and comprehensive foundation for future learning.

Parents, we yearn for nothing more than to see our children thrive academically and personally. We want to witness the spark of inspiration ignited within them as they overcome academic challenges with confidence and poise. Summer Bridge Building Activities books serve as indispensable partners in this noble endeavor, offering not just practice questions but the keys to unlocking a world of academic and personal opportunities.

Visualize the pride on your child's face as they master a challenging math concept, the joy they experience when their efforts yield results, and the confidence they gain with each success. These pages are designed to make learning math a positive, enriching, and deeply rewarding experience that will benefit them throughout their academic journey and beyond.

For educators, Summer Bridge Building Activities books are invaluable allies in the quest to cultivate mathematical proficiency in the classroom. Accompanied by comprehensive guides and readily available answers, instructors can focus on mentoring and nurturing their students, secure in the knowledge that these books provide a robust framework for effective learning.

Within the pages of Summer Bridge Building Activities books lies not just the promise of academic excellence, but the seeds of a brighter future. By integrating these resources into your child's summer routine, you are bestowing upon them the gifts of confidence, curiosity, and a lifelong love of learning.

Invest in your child's future today with Summer Bridge Building Activities books — because every great journey begins with a single step, and this step can change everything. Keep the momentum of learning alive over the summer, and watch your child soar to new academic heights.

Contents

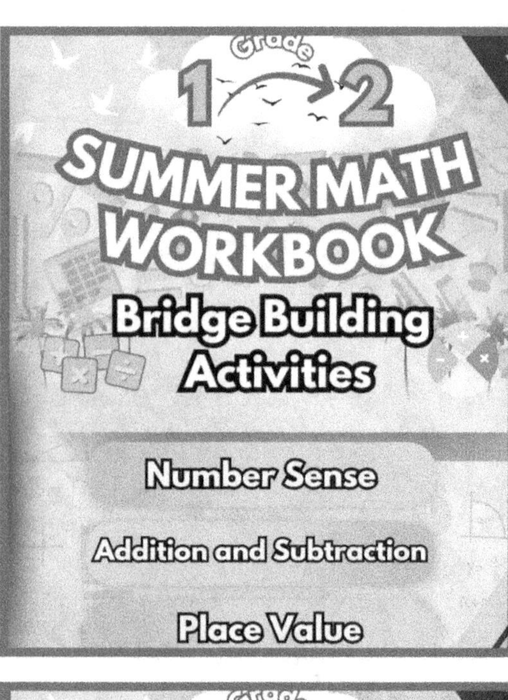

Grade
1 2
SUMMER MATH WORKBOOK
Bridge Building Activities
Number Sense
Addition and Subtraction
Place Value

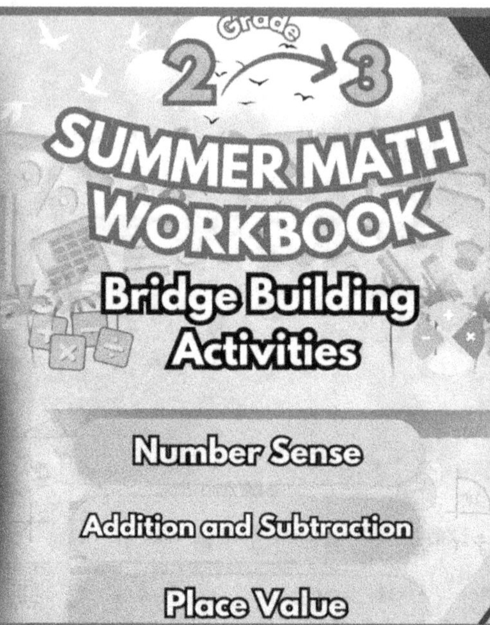

Grade
2 3
SUMMER MATH WORKBOOK
Bridge Building Activities
Number Sense
Addition and Subtraction
Place Value

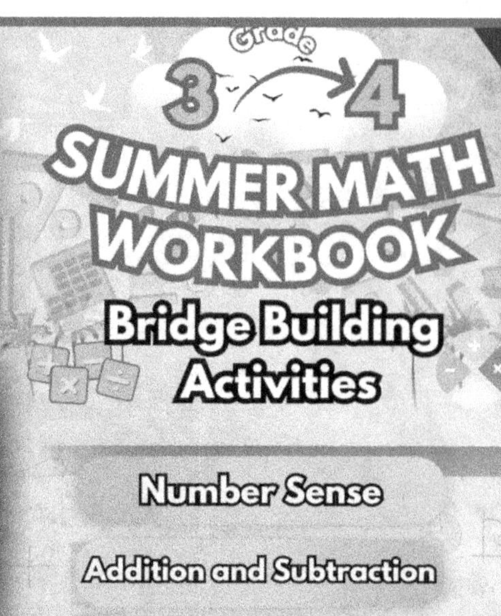

Grade
3 4
SUMMER MATH WORKBOOK
Bridge Building Activities
Number Sense
Addition and Subtraction
Place Value

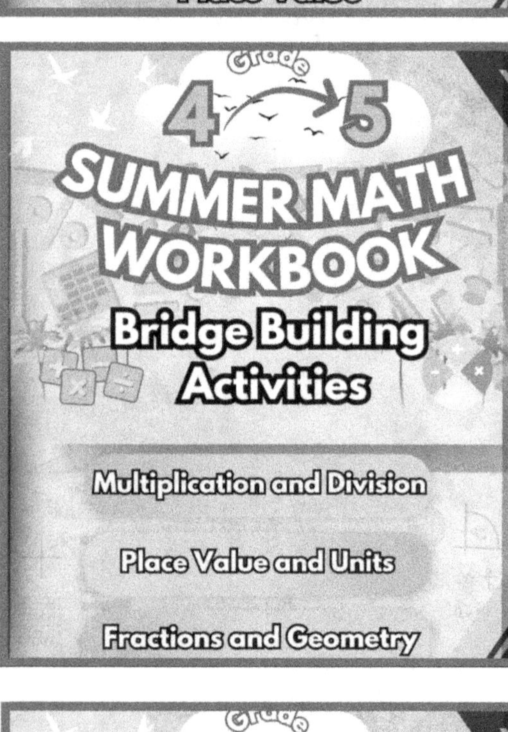

Grade
4 5
SUMMER MATH WORKBOOK
Bridge Building Activities
Multiplication and Division
Place Value and Units
Fractions and Geometry

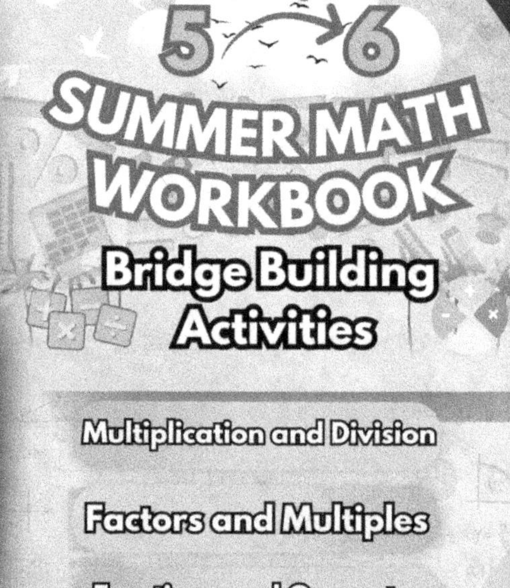

Grade
5 6
SUMMER MATH WORKBOOK
Bridge Building Activities
Multiplication and Division
Factors and Multiples
Fractions and Geometry

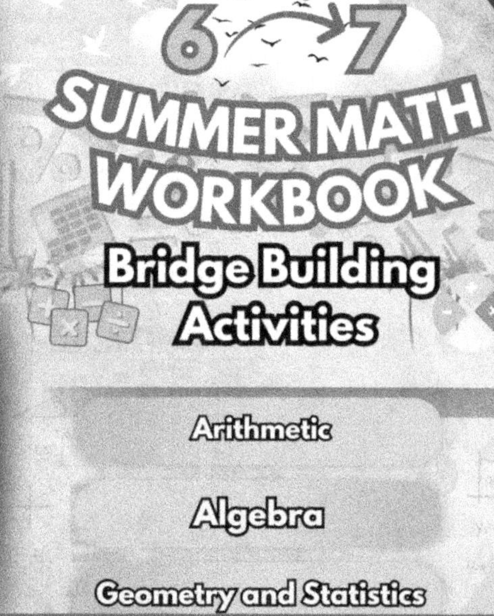

Grade
6 7
SUMMER MATH WORKBOOK
Bridge Building Activities
Arithmetic
Algebra
Geometry and Statistics

Grade
7 8
SUMMER MATH WORKBOOK
Bridge Building Activities
Ratio and Percentage
Algebra and Cartesian Plane
Geometry and Statistics

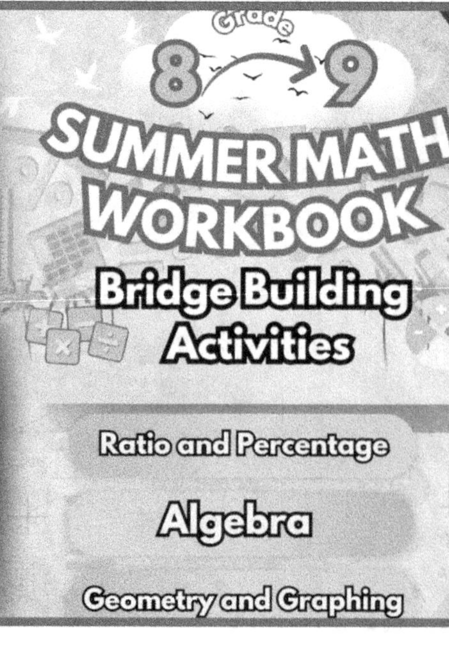

Grade
8 9
SUMMER MATH WORKBOOK
Bridge Building Activities
Ratio and Percentage
Algebra
Geometry and Graphing

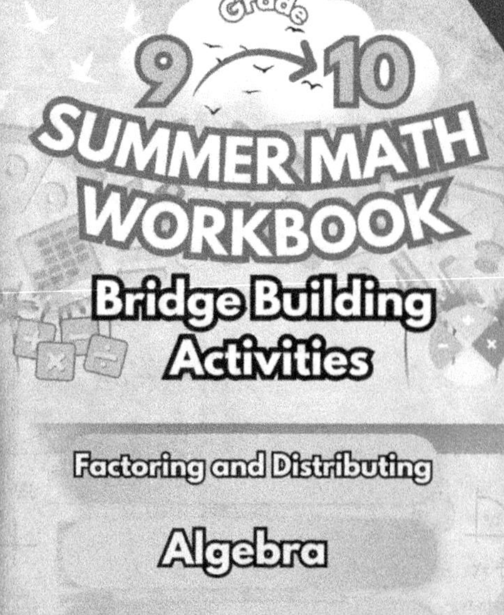

Grade
9 10
SUMMER MATH WORKBOOK
Bridge Building Activities
Factoring and Distributing
Algebra
Geometry and Graphing

<u>**Compare the Numbers**</u>

We use words like "greater than," "less than," and "equal to" to compare numbers.

- Greater than (>) means a number is bigger.

- Less than (<) means a number is smaller.

- Equal to (=) means two numbers are the same.

Example:

5 is greater than 3 (5 > 3)

10 is less than 12 (10 < 12)

7 is equal to 7 (7 = 7)

<u>**Circle the Numbers**</u>

In a group of numbers, the smallest number is the one with the least value, and the largest number is the one with the greatest value.

Example:

Circle the smallest and largest numbers:

2, 7, 1, 9, 4

- **Smallest:** 1

- **Largest:** 9

Odd and Even Numbers

- **Even numbers** are whole numbers that can be divided by 2 evenly, with no remainder. They always end in 0, 2, 4, 6, or 8.

- **Odd numbers** are whole numbers that cannot be divided by 2 evenly. They always end in 1, 3, 5, 7, or 9.

Example:

Identify the odd and even numbers:

6, 9, 12, 15, 20

- **Even:** 6, 12, 20

- **Odd:** 9, 15

Missing Numbers

The numbers always follow same sequence. In this activity, some sequence of numbers is given, and the task is to find the numbers that come before, between and after those numbers.

Example:

43, _____ , 45

the missing number is 44.

Addition and Subtraction

Addition

Addition means putting numbers together to find the total.

Example:

What is 5 + 3?

Imagine you have 5 toy cars, and you get 3 more. How many toy cars do you have now?

$$5 + 3 = 8$$

You have 8 toy cars!

$$\mathbf{2 + 3 = 5}$$

Subtraction

Subtraction means taking away a number from another to find the difference.

Example:

What is 10 - 4?

Imagine you have 10 candies, and you give 4 away. How many candies do you have left?

$$10 - 4 = 6$$

You have 6 candies left!

Place Value

Place value helps us determine the worth of each digit in a number.

Consider the number **842**. It consists of three digits: 8, 4, and 2.

Digit	Place Value Position	Value Calculation	Value
8	Hundreds place	8 × 100	800
4	Tens place	4 × 10	40
2	Ones place	2 × 1	2

Each digit occupies a unique position:

- The digit **8** is in the hundreds place, signifying eight groups of 100.

- The digit **4** is in the tens place, indicating four groups of 10.

- The digit **2** is in the ones place, representing two single units.

To find the total value of the number **842**, we calculate the value of each digit based on its place:

- The digit **8** in the hundreds place equals 800.

- The digit **4** in the tens place equals 40.

- The digit **2** in the ones place equals 2.

By summing these values, we determine the overall value of the number:

$$800 + 40 + 2 = 842$$

Counting Up and Down

Fill in the missing numbers by counting Up and Down.

1.

546	547	548	549	550

2.

754				758

3.

	45	46		

4.

			75	74

5.

		747	748	

6.

17	18			

7.

823				819

8.

		152		150

9.

			736	735

10.

		358	359	

11.

			562	563

12.

	282			279

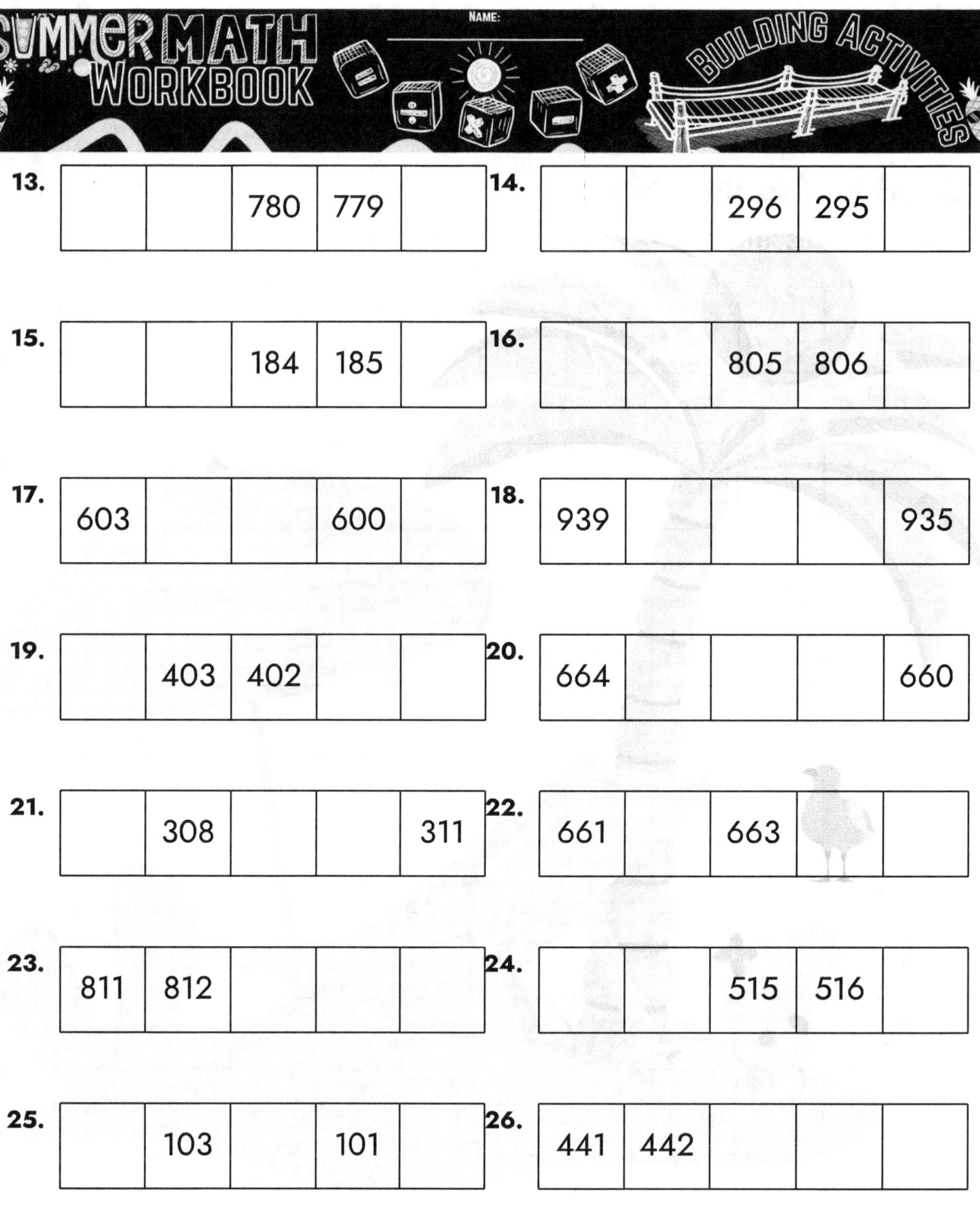

13. | | | 780 | 779 | |

14. | | | 296 | 295 | |

15. | | | 184 | 185 | |

16. | | | 805 | 806 | |

17. | 603 | | | 600 | |

18. | 939 | | | | 935 |

19. | | 403 | 402 | | |

20. | 664 | | | | 660 |

21. | | 308 | | | 311 |

22. | 661 | | 663 | | |

23. | 811 | 812 | | | |

24. | | | 515 | 516 | |

25. | | 103 | | 101 | |

26. | 441 | 442 | | | |

Counting Patterns: Count by 2s to 5s

Complete the counting tables.

1. Count by 2 from 427 to 435

427	429	431	433	435

2. Count by 2 from 600 to 608

	602			

3. Count by 4 from 191 to 207

		199		

4. Count by 2 from 316 to 324

	318			

5. Count by 2 from 596 to 604

		600		

6. Count by 2 from 933 to 941

	935			

7. Count by 3 from 300 to 312

300				

8. Count by 3 from 315 to 327

315				

9. Count by 2 from 751 to 759

		755		

10. Count by 4 from 573 to 589

573				

11. Count by 5 from 733 to 753

	738			

12. Count by 2 from 882 to 890

882				

13. Count by 2 from 171 to 179

	173			

14. Count by 2 from 886 to 894

	888			

15. Count by 4 from 468 to 484

468				

16. Count by 4 from 919 to 935

919				

17. Count by 5 from 952 to 972

		962		

18. Count by 5 from 320 to 340

		330		

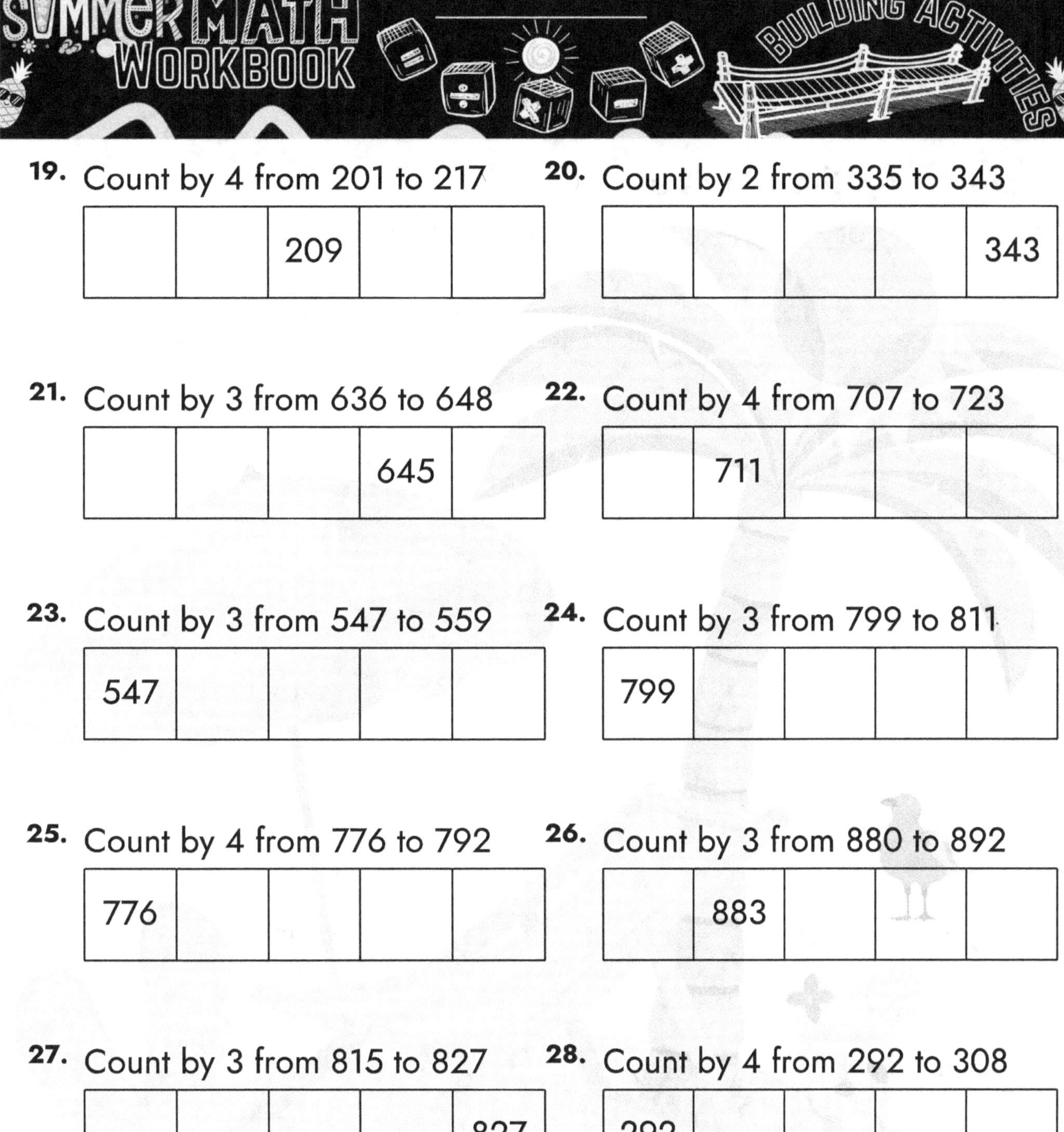

19. Count by 4 from 201 to 217

		209		

20. Count by 2 from 335 to 343

				343

21. Count by 3 from 636 to 648

			645	

22. Count by 4 from 707 to 723

	711			

23. Count by 3 from 547 to 559

547				

24. Count by 3 from 799 to 811

799				

25. Count by 4 from 776 to 792

776				

26. Count by 3 from 880 to 892

		883		

27. Count by 3 from 815 to 827

				827

28. Count by 4 from 292 to 308

292				

Comparing the Numbers

Add: > or < or = to make the following statements true.

1. 118 < 971

2. 334 ____ 563

3. 618 ____ 317

4. 812 ____ 827

5. 344 ____ 683

6. 942 ____ 714

7. 817 ____ 203

8. 223 ____ 348

9. 128 ____ 504

10. 846 ____ 421

11. 380 ____ 798

12. 161 ____ 245

13. 518 ____ 853

14. 786 ____ 213

15. 666 ____ 412

16. 476 ____ 240

17. 137 _______ 349

18. 525 _______ 180

19. 182 _______ 906

20. 357 _______ 942

21. 508 _______ 272

22. 407 _______ 512

23. 824 _______ 343

24. 601 _______ 519

25. 868 _______ 432

26. 206 _______ 384

27. 898 _______ 116

28. 168 _______ 320

29. 910 _______ 188

30. 144 _______ 765

31. 531 _______ 699

32. 261 _______ 932

33. 307 _______ 802

34. 677 _______ 568

35. 677 _______ 142

36. 266 _______ 222

37. 246 _______ 904

38. 912 _______ 207

39. 490 _______ 648

40. 421 _______ 275

41. 351 _______ 366

42. 344 _______ 334

43. 306 _______ 191

44. 341 _______ 121

45. 280 _______ 305

46. 270 _______ 993

47. 862 _______ 592

48. 510 _______ 808

49. 111 _______ 475

50. 304 _______ 122

51. 665 _______ 133

52. 841 _______ 826

Circle the Numbers

Circle the smallest number in each group.

1. 564 461 (252) 274

2. 915 277 301 641

3. 414 989 51 398

4. 10 392 275 840

5. 499 623 589 732

6. 694 646 415 758

7. 895 772 518 799

8. 685 372 968 100

9. 592 660 600 263

10. 759 22 369 543

11. 256 882 650 527

12. 34 156 401 327

13. 635 551 126 368

14. 252 971 174 917

15. 47 494 378 143

16. 759 501 956 42

17. 21 950 805 349

18. 792 12 82 477

19. 254 47 477 811

20. 996 888 725 740

21. 372 191 165 134

22. 247 600 847 621

23. 486 682 217 265

24. 643 227 783 755

25. 926 608 506 83

26. 350 52 534 623

27. 470 648 114 206

28. 494 363 921 159

29. 769 638 771 568

30. 337 823 795 420

31. 103 184 862 110

32. 795 816 833 28

Circle the Numbers

Circle the biggest number in each group.

1. 264   722   (885)   388

2. 382   642   390   320

3. 657   541   663   599

4. 486   642   127   124

5. 760   59   496   6

6. 455   215   418   104

7. 813   86   979   166

8. 189   425   828   654

9. 814   87   941   772

10. 477   534   776   127

11. 248   451   911   796

12. 160   197   934   461

13. 58   739   349   737

14. 320   828   572   49

15. 304   781   574   297

16. 662   224   132   233

17. 712   10   784   400

18. 701   355   646   227

19. 282   370   758   5

20. 304   622   943   617

21. 152   519   109   450

22. 76   92   334   986

23. 514   892   468   695

24. 959   480   465   24

25. 320   679   84   151

26. 412   534   759   702

27. 93   123   455   950

28. 70   568   745   681

29. 838   957   145   143

30. 116   681   157   621

31. 675   798   886   808

32. 886   950   267   802

Circle the Numbers

Circle the smallest and biggest number in each group.

1. (904) 734 685 (625)
2. 539 793 205 618

3. 759 407 357 952
4. 636 384 916 946

5. 148 786 857 2
6. 335 322 908 638

7. 522 462 475 614
8. 647 951 815 143

9. 855 652 46 336
10. 882 121 143 45

11. 753 527 383 709
12. 325 205 984 291

13. 881 940 660 100
14. 93 266 468 583

15. 826 47 103 77
16. 318 590 970 808

17. 591 215 98 984

18. 339 580 64 28

19. 644 812 249 808

20. 939 200 314 318

21. 478 185 732 707

22. 291 715 50 590

23. 185 463 510 835

24. 18 67 727 163

25. 556 575 118 110

26. 108 1 952 301

27. 876 633 456 281

28. 17 660 643 626

29. 733 785 598 133

30. 858 263 517 875

31. 165 507 799 876

32. 71 229 11 578

Circle the Numbers

Circle the odd numbers in each group.

1. 86 252 364 82

2. 204 (211) 478 (233)

3. 431 831 658 260

4. 769 573 525 819

5. 883 103 232 468

6. 594 305 293 58

7. 243 945 600 201

8. 76 231 648 623

9. 878 196 930 408

10. 280 544 529 575

11. 121 900 427 432

12. 859 615 396 933

13. 275 57 187 127

14. 778 110 491 781

15. 958 307 839 259

16. 610 277 157 201

17. 184 35 382 574

18. 642 117 540 339

19. 573 656 347 694

20. 877 861 198 627

21. 549 667 925 19

22. 45 521 844 768

23. 704 150 450 972

24. 705 271 965 844

25. 743 227 249 825

26. 234 822 291 159

27. 517 847 553 123

28. 763 797 904 97

29. 110 212 709 943

30. 351 138 157 662

31. 191 613 869 493

32. 666 567 634 302

Circle the Numbers

Circle the even numbers in each group.

1. 691   503   950   650

2. 613   373   393   727

3. 376   767   502   197

4. 967   722   6   907

5. 245   353   863   493

6. 562   23   493   606

7. 71   586   634   620

8. 952   797   492   950

9. 214   252   431   260

10. 846   254   484   736

11. 818   981   567   584

12. 636   959   694   469

13. 608   961   249   314

14. 704   141   740   669

15. 10   345   580   27

16. 738   773   774   578

17. 276 552 983 716

18. 291 745 61 990

19. 869 127 675 580

20. 455 909 969 112

21. 891 166 13 990

22. 549 179 247 73

23. 512 762 250 502

24. 674 457 998 46

25. 207 988 308 85

26. 976 978 179 862

27. 901 258 444 577

28. 466 160 214 101

29. 375 468 135 572

30. 760 783 30 97

31. 306 910 205 528

32. 495 559 317 412

Missing Numbers: Before and After

1. 849   850   851

2. _______ 762 _______

3. _______ 672 _______

4. _______ 910 _______

5. _______ 943 _______

6. _______ 495 _______

7. _______ 242 _______

Missing Numbers: Between

1. 128 _______ 130

2. 373 _______ 375

3. 601 _______ 603

4. 135 _______ 137

5. 987 _______ 989

6. 90 _______ 92

7. 734 _______ 736

8. _________ 385 _________

9. _________ 82 _________

10. _________ 829 _________

11. _________ 390 _________

12. _________ 417 _________

13. _________ 289 _________

14. _________ 697 _________

15. _________ 239 _________

8. 607 _________ 609

9. 549 _________ 551

10. 127 _________ 129

11. 322 _________ 324

12. 286 _________ 288

13. 959 _________ 961

14. 779 _________ 781

15. 773 _________ 775

16. _______ 861 _______　　**16.** 368 _______ 370

17. _______ 221 _______　　**17.** 941 _______ 943

18. _______ 541 _______　　**18.** 449 _______ 451

19. _______ 309 _______　　**19.** 787 _______ 789

20. _______ 667 _______　　**20.** 500 _______ 502

21. _______ 839 _______　　**21.** 333 _______ 335

22. _______ 761 _______　　**22.** 585 _______ 587

23. _______ 277 _______　　**23.** 693 _______ 695

24. ______ 561 ______

25. ______ 254 ______

26. ______ 21 ______

27. ______ 848 ______

28. ______ 833 ______

29. ______ 728 ______

30. ______ 634 ______

31. ______ 327 ______

24. 363 ______ 365

25. 304 ______ 306

26. 979 ______ 981

27. 432 ______ 434

28. 343 ______ 345

29. 507 ______ 509

30. 106 ______ 108

31. 141 ______ 143

32. ______ 594 ______   **32.** 782 ______ 784

33. ______ 887 ______   **33.** 350 ______ 352

34. ______ 619 ______   **34.** 220 ______ 222

35. ______ 571 ______   **35.** 565 ______ 567

36. ______ 956 ______   **36.** 649 ______ 651

37. ______ 582 ______   **37.** 872 ______ 874

38. ______ 109 ______   **38.** 841 ______ 843

39. ______ 901 ______   **39.** 730 ______ 732

Addition 1 to 20

Find the Sum.

1. 6
+ 12
____
18

2. 13
+ 4
____

3. 11
+ 13
____

4. 19
+ 6
____

5. 17
+ 9
____

6. 10
+ 8
____

7. 5
+ 3
____

8. 12
+ 4
____

9. 9
+ 15
____

10. 19
+ 16
____

11. 12
+ 10
____

12. 3
+ 13
____

13. 19
+ 17
____

14. 1
+ 16
____

15. 14
+ 19
____

16. 6
+ 16
____

17. 19
+ 2
____

18. 18
+ 4
____

19. 12
+ 19
____

20. 20
+ 13
____

21. 1
+ 4
____

22. 10
+ 5
____

23. 5
+ 18
____

24. 6
+ 9
____

25. 13
+ 8
____

26. $\begin{array}{r} 19 \\ +\ 3 \\ \hline \end{array}$	27. $\begin{array}{r} 8 \\ +16 \\ \hline \end{array}$	28. $\begin{array}{r} 10 \\ +\ 1 \\ \hline \end{array}$	29. $\begin{array}{r} 5 \\ +15 \\ \hline \end{array}$	30. $\begin{array}{r} 20 \\ +16 \\ \hline \end{array}$
31. $\begin{array}{r} 6 \\ +\ 2 \\ \hline \end{array}$	32. $\begin{array}{r} 15 \\ +10 \\ \hline \end{array}$	33. $\begin{array}{r} 2 \\ +10 \\ \hline \end{array}$	34. $\begin{array}{r} 3 \\ +11 \\ \hline \end{array}$	35. $\begin{array}{r} 7 \\ +\ 6 \\ \hline \end{array}$
36. $\begin{array}{r} 4 \\ +19 \\ \hline \end{array}$	37. $\begin{array}{r} 17 \\ +19 \\ \hline \end{array}$	38. $\begin{array}{r} 9 \\ +19 \\ \hline \end{array}$	39. $\begin{array}{r} 3 \\ +15 \\ \hline \end{array}$	40. $\begin{array}{r} 13 \\ +16 \\ \hline \end{array}$
41. $\begin{array}{r} 18 \\ +12 \\ \hline \end{array}$	42. $\begin{array}{r} 4 \\ +\ 7 \\ \hline \end{array}$	43. $\begin{array}{r} 1 \\ +\ 5 \\ \hline \end{array}$	44. $\begin{array}{r} 9 \\ +\ 4 \\ \hline \end{array}$	45. $\begin{array}{r} 13 \\ +17 \\ \hline \end{array}$
46. $\begin{array}{r} 20 \\ +17 \\ \hline \end{array}$	47. $\begin{array}{r} 20 \\ +\ 4 \\ \hline \end{array}$	48. $\begin{array}{r} 8 \\ +19 \\ \hline \end{array}$	49. $\begin{array}{r} 9 \\ +\ 1 \\ \hline \end{array}$	50. $\begin{array}{r} 4 \\ +15 \\ \hline \end{array}$

Double Digit Addition

Find the Sum.

1.
```
  78
+ 78
-----
 156
```

2.
```
  20
+ 43
-----
```

3.
```
  30
+ 98
-----
```

4.
```
  34
+ 45
-----
```

5.
```
  42
+ 57
-----
```

6.
```
  91
+ 49
-----
```

7.
```
  16
+ 28
-----
```

8.
```
  92
+ 68
-----
```

9.
```
  90
+ 51
-----
```

10.
```
  52
+ 87
-----
```

11.
```
  12
+ 95
-----
```

12.
```
  90
+ 49
-----
```

13.
```
  35
+ 36
-----
```

14.
```
  96
+ 68
-----
```

15.
```
  64
+ 53
-----
```

16.
```
  55
+ 19
-----
```

17.
```
  63
+ 91
-----
```

18.
```
  11
+ 21
-----
```

19.
```
  54
+ 80
-----
```

20.
```
  16
+ 13
-----
```

21.
```
  92
+ 14
-----
```

22.
```
  81
+ 18
-----
```

23.
```
  95
+ 59
-----
```

24.
```
  81
+ 81
-----
```

25.
```
  32
+ 73
-----
```

26. $\begin{array}{r} 16 \\ +\ 95 \\ \hline \end{array}$	**27.** $\begin{array}{r} 57 \\ +\ 36 \\ \hline \end{array}$	**28.** $\begin{array}{r} 73 \\ +\ 82 \\ \hline \end{array}$	**29.** $\begin{array}{r} 87 \\ +\ 70 \\ \hline \end{array}$	**30.** $\begin{array}{r} 17 \\ +\ 93 \\ \hline \end{array}$
31. $\begin{array}{r} 11 \\ +\ 65 \\ \hline \end{array}$	**32.** $\begin{array}{r} 80 \\ +\ 89 \\ \hline \end{array}$	**33.** $\begin{array}{r} 12 \\ +\ 82 \\ \hline \end{array}$	**34.** $\begin{array}{r} 85 \\ +\ 23 \\ \hline \end{array}$	**35.** $\begin{array}{r} 26 \\ +\ 81 \\ \hline \end{array}$
36. $\begin{array}{r} 24 \\ +\ 20 \\ \hline \end{array}$	**37.** $\begin{array}{r} 46 \\ +\ 49 \\ \hline \end{array}$	**38.** $\begin{array}{r} 94 \\ +\ 98 \\ \hline \end{array}$	**39.** $\begin{array}{r} 24 \\ +\ 81 \\ \hline \end{array}$	**40.** $\begin{array}{r} 53 \\ +\ 76 \\ \hline \end{array}$
41. $\begin{array}{r} 55 \\ +\ 26 \\ \hline \end{array}$	**42.** $\begin{array}{r} 46 \\ +\ 89 \\ \hline \end{array}$	**43.** $\begin{array}{r} 47 \\ +\ 58 \\ \hline \end{array}$	**44.** $\begin{array}{r} 60 \\ +\ 37 \\ \hline \end{array}$	**45.** $\begin{array}{r} 28 \\ +\ 29 \\ \hline \end{array}$
46. $\begin{array}{r} 33 \\ +\ 83 \\ \hline \end{array}$	**47.** $\begin{array}{r} 72 \\ +\ 22 \\ \hline \end{array}$	**48.** $\begin{array}{r} 12 \\ +\ 37 \\ \hline \end{array}$	**49.** $\begin{array}{r} 33 \\ +\ 91 \\ \hline \end{array}$	**50.** $\begin{array}{r} 16 \\ +\ 24 \\ \hline \end{array}$

Subtraction 1 to 20

Find the Difference.

1. 14
  − 9
  ——
    5

2. 13
  − 6

3. 12
  − 12

4. 12
  − 2

5. 8
  − 6

6. 13
  − 2

7. 5
  − 2

8. 9
  − 8

9. 5
  − 5

10. 10
   − 5

11. 6
   − 4

12. 19
   − 18

13. 11
   − 4

14. 9
   − 3

15. 9
   − 6

16. 15
   − 4

17. 15
   − 6

18. 2
   − 2

19. 7
   − 4

20. 20
   − 10

21.	22.	23.	24.	25.
19 − 10	12 − 3	13 − 5	14 − 3	3 − 2

26.	27.	28.	29.	30.
18 − 4	18 − 5	14 − 10	20 − 9	7 − 6

31.	32.	33.	34.	35.
6 − 2	12 − 1	11 − 9	12 − 6	9 − 4

36.	37.	38.	39.	40.
14 − 2	12 − 4	11 − 5	16 − 3	4 − 4

41.	42.	43.	44.	45.
2 − 1	18 − 13	16 − 5	10 − 2	17 − 13

Double Digit Subtraction

Find the Difference.

1. 14 − 11 ___ 3	**2.** 92 − 78	**3.** 82 − 40	**4.** 18 − 11	**5.** 63 − 23
6. 31 − 22	**7.** 57 − 33	**8.** 74 − 38	**9.** 25 − 19	**10.** 63 − 20
11. 50 − 28	**12.** 47 − 23	**13.** 28 − 18	**14.** 20 − 18	**15.** 96 − 39
16. 97 − 32	**17.** 53 − 50	**18.** 11 − 10	**19.** 38 − 30	**20.** 60 − 29

21. $\begin{array}{r} 15 \\ -\ 11 \\ \hline \end{array}$	**22.** $\begin{array}{r} 34 \\ -\ 32 \\ \hline \end{array}$	**23.** $\begin{array}{r} 72 \\ -\ 41 \\ \hline \end{array}$	**24.** $\begin{array}{r} 62 \\ -\ 32 \\ \hline \end{array}$	**25.** $\begin{array}{r} 97 \\ -\ 42 \\ \hline \end{array}$
26. $\begin{array}{r} 16 \\ -\ 15 \\ \hline \end{array}$	**27.** $\begin{array}{r} 60 \\ -\ 43 \\ \hline \end{array}$	**28.** $\begin{array}{r} 37 \\ -\ 26 \\ \hline \end{array}$	**29.** $\begin{array}{r} 74 \\ -\ 47 \\ \hline \end{array}$	**30.** $\begin{array}{r} 66 \\ -\ 30 \\ \hline \end{array}$
31. $\begin{array}{r} 37 \\ -\ 18 \\ \hline \end{array}$	**32.** $\begin{array}{r} 27 \\ -\ 14 \\ \hline \end{array}$	**33.** $\begin{array}{r} 33 \\ -\ 32 \\ \hline \end{array}$	**34.** $\begin{array}{r} 16 \\ -\ 13 \\ \hline \end{array}$	**35.** $\begin{array}{r} 53 \\ -\ 22 \\ \hline \end{array}$
36. $\begin{array}{r} 21 \\ -\ 15 \\ \hline \end{array}$	**37.** $\begin{array}{r} 16 \\ -\ 11 \\ \hline \end{array}$	**38.** $\begin{array}{r} 22 \\ -\ 12 \\ \hline \end{array}$	**39.** $\begin{array}{r} 27 \\ -\ 18 \\ \hline \end{array}$	**40.** $\begin{array}{r} 68 \\ -\ 51 \\ \hline \end{array}$
41. $\begin{array}{r} 87 \\ -\ 64 \\ \hline \end{array}$	**42.** $\begin{array}{r} 84 \\ -\ 54 \\ \hline \end{array}$	**43.** $\begin{array}{r} 34 \\ -\ 13 \\ \hline \end{array}$	**44.** $\begin{array}{r} 72 \\ -\ 61 \\ \hline \end{array}$	**45.** $\begin{array}{r} 67 \\ -\ 34 \\ \hline \end{array}$

46.
$$74 - 58$$

47.
$$17 - 11$$

48.
$$17 - 15$$

49.
$$17 - 10$$

50.
$$69 - 52$$

51.
$$49 - 10$$

52.
$$93 - 68$$

53.
$$32 - 23$$

54.
$$80 - 34$$

55.
$$57 - 15$$

56.
$$46 - 18$$

57.
$$92 - 86$$

58.
$$53 - 36$$

59.
$$50 - 34$$

60.
$$97 - 23$$

61.
$$36 - 16$$

62.
$$94 - 15$$

63.
$$59 - 29$$

64.
$$44 - 39$$

65.
$$22 - 14$$

66.
$$20 - 12$$

67.
$$83 - 78$$

68.
$$34 - 31$$

69.
$$78 - 19$$

70.
$$42 - 31$$

71.	72.	73.	74.	75.
39 − 20	36 − 24	83 − 21	74 − 40	40 − 25

76.	77.	78.	79.	80.
13 − 12	48 − 17	15 − 14	23 − 21	30 − 29

81.	82.	83.	84.	85.
29 − 13	10 − 10	47 − 47	69 − 46	85 − 33

86.	87.	88.	89.	90.
31 − 17	83 − 79	95 − 46	14 − 10	60 − 21

91.	92.	93.	94.	95.
22 − 18	12 − 11	23 − 14	55 − 14	82 − 75

Addition - Doubles

Find the sum.

1. $\begin{array}{r} 54 \\ +\ 54 \\ \hline 108 \end{array}$	**2.** $\begin{array}{r} 46 \\ +\ 46 \\ \hline \end{array}$	**3.** $\begin{array}{r} 20 \\ +\ 20 \\ \hline \end{array}$	**4.** $\begin{array}{r} 80 \\ +\ 80 \\ \hline \end{array}$
5. $\begin{array}{r} 84 \\ +\ 84 \\ \hline \end{array}$	**6.** $\begin{array}{r} 19 \\ +\ 19 \\ \hline \end{array}$	**7.** $\begin{array}{r} 12 \\ +\ 12 \\ \hline \end{array}$	**8.** $\begin{array}{r} 74 \\ +\ 74 \\ \hline \end{array}$
9. $\begin{array}{r} 53 \\ +\ 53 \\ \hline \end{array}$	**10.** $\begin{array}{r} 66 \\ +\ 66 \\ \hline \end{array}$	**11.** $\begin{array}{r} 17 \\ +\ 17 \\ \hline \end{array}$	**12.** $\begin{array}{r} 10 \\ +\ 10 \\ \hline \end{array}$
13. $\begin{array}{r} 59 \\ +\ 59 \\ \hline \end{array}$	**14.** $\begin{array}{r} 43 \\ +\ 43 \\ \hline \end{array}$	**15.** $\begin{array}{r} 62 \\ +\ 62 \\ \hline \end{array}$	**16.** $\begin{array}{r} 94 \\ +\ 94 \\ \hline \end{array}$

17. 76 + 76	**18.** 47 + 47	**19.** 85 + 85	**20.** 33 + 33
21. 75 + 75	**22.** 13 + 13	**23.** 48 + 48	**24.** 26 + 26
25. 91 + 91	**26.** 49 + 49	**27.** 23 + 23	**28.** 96 + 96
29. 71 + 71	**30.** 55 + 55	**31.** 36 + 36	**32.** 45 + 45
33. 61 + 61	**34.** 77 + 77	**35.** 68 + 68	**36.** 51 + 51

37. $\begin{array}{r} 31 \\ +\ 31 \\ \hline \end{array}$	**38.** $\begin{array}{r} 78 \\ +\ 78 \\ \hline \end{array}$	**39.** $\begin{array}{r} 11 \\ +\ 11 \\ \hline \end{array}$	**40.** $\begin{array}{r} 83 \\ +\ 83 \\ \hline \end{array}$
41. $\begin{array}{r} 41 \\ +\ 41 \\ \hline \end{array}$	**42.** $\begin{array}{r} 87 \\ +\ 87 \\ \hline \end{array}$	**43.** $\begin{array}{r} 37 \\ +\ 37 \\ \hline \end{array}$	**44.** $\begin{array}{r} 50 \\ +\ 50 \\ \hline \end{array}$
45. $\begin{array}{r} 65 \\ +\ 65 \\ \hline \end{array}$	**46.** $\begin{array}{r} 86 \\ +\ 86 \\ \hline \end{array}$	**47.** $\begin{array}{r} 16 \\ +\ 16 \\ \hline \end{array}$	**48.** $\begin{array}{r} 89 \\ +\ 89 \\ \hline \end{array}$
49. $\begin{array}{r} 70 \\ +\ 70 \\ \hline \end{array}$	**50.** $\begin{array}{r} 95 \\ +\ 95 \\ \hline \end{array}$	**51.** $\begin{array}{r} 18 \\ +\ 18 \\ \hline \end{array}$	**52.** $\begin{array}{r} 24 \\ +\ 24 \\ \hline \end{array}$
53. $\begin{array}{r} 21 \\ +\ 21 \\ \hline \end{array}$	**54.** $\begin{array}{r} 28 \\ +\ 28 \\ \hline \end{array}$	**55.** $\begin{array}{r} 93 \\ +\ 93 \\ \hline \end{array}$	**56.** $\begin{array}{r} 15 \\ +\ 15 \\ \hline \end{array}$

Fact Families: Addition and Subtraction

Complete each family of facts.

1.

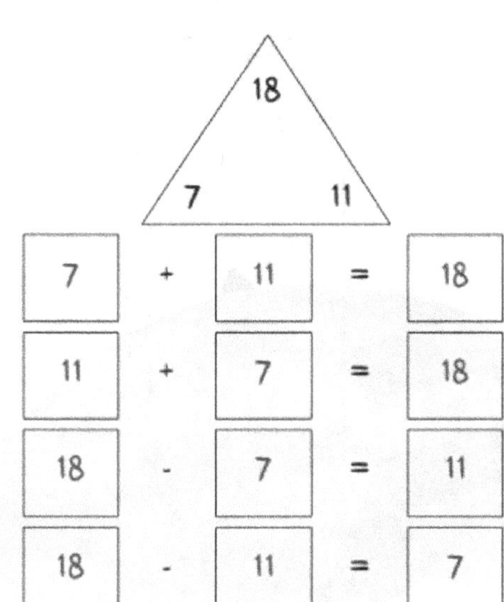

18 / 7   11

7	+	11	=	18
11	+	7	=	18
18	-	7	=	11
18	-	11	=	7

2.

25 / 15   10

	+		=	
	+		=	
	-		=	
	-		=	

3.

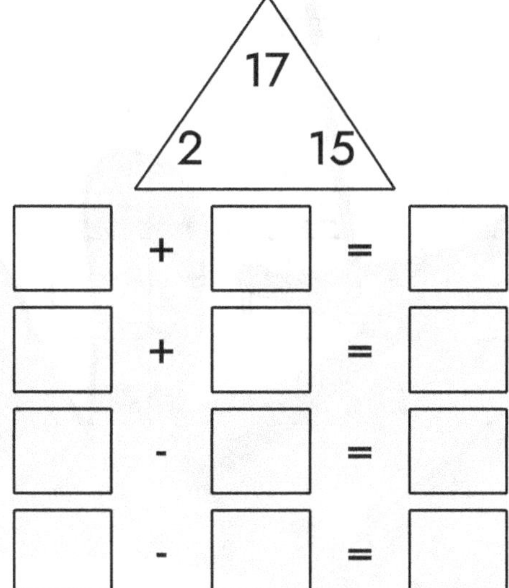

17 / 2   15

	+		=	
	+		=	
	-		=	
	-		=	

4.

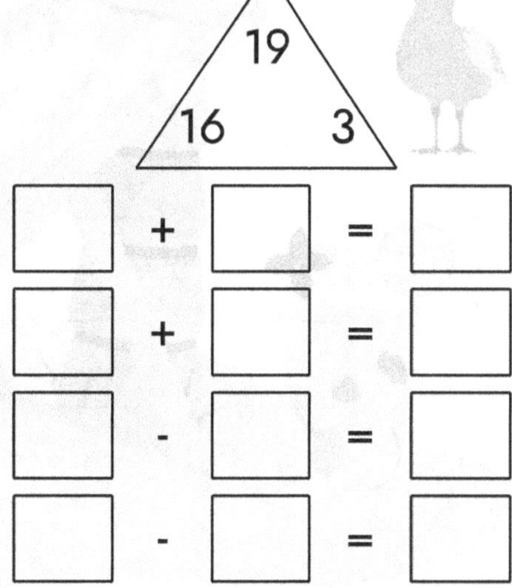

19 / 16   3

	+		=	
	+		=	
	-		=	
	-		=	

SUMMER MATH WORKBOOK
BUILDING ACTIVITIES
NAME:

5.

22
8   14

☐ + ☐ = ☐
☐ + ☐ = ☐
☐ - ☐ = ☐
☐ - ☐ = ☐

6.

18
16   2

☐ + ☐ = ☐
☐ + ☐ = ☐
☐ - ☐ = ☐
☐ - ☐ = ☐

7.

20
7   13

☐ + ☐ = ☐
☐ + ☐ = ☐
☐ - ☐ = ☐
☐ - ☐ = ☐

8.

14
12   2

☐ + ☐ = ☐
☐ + ☐ = ☐
☐ - ☐ = ☐
☐ - ☐ = ☐

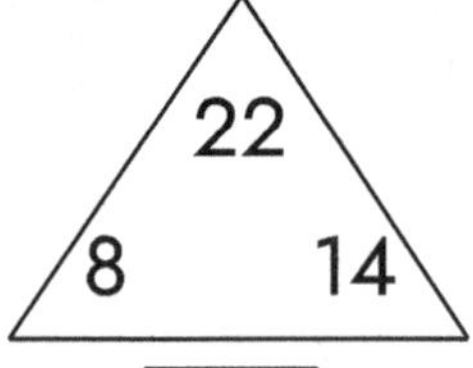

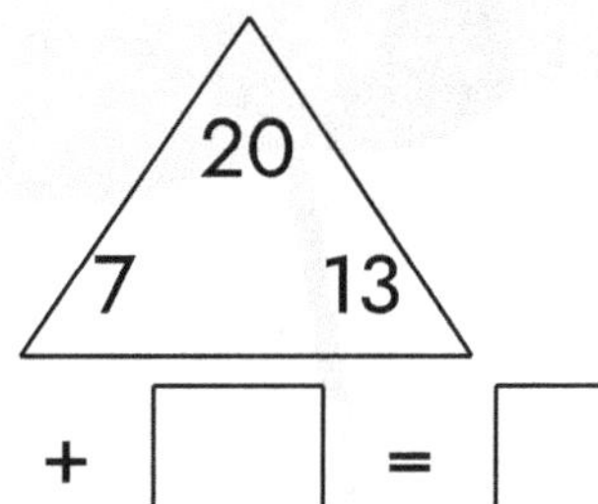

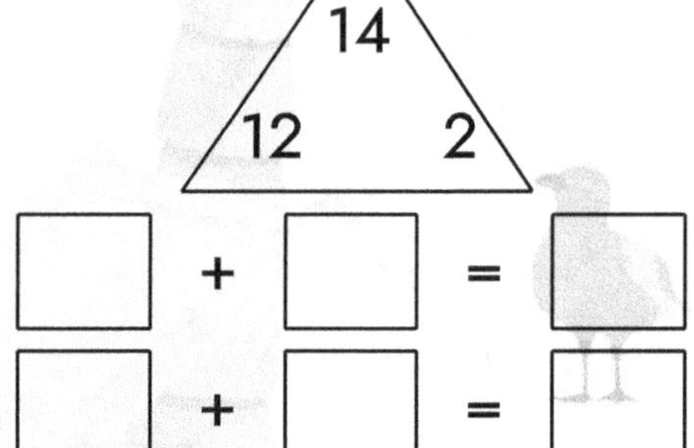

9.

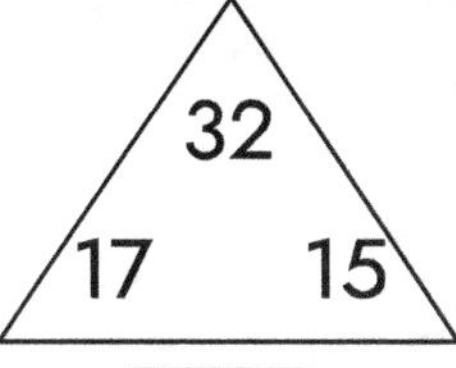

[ ] + [ ] = [ ]

[ ] + [ ] = [ ]

[ ] - [ ] = [ ]

[ ] - [ ] = [ ]

10.

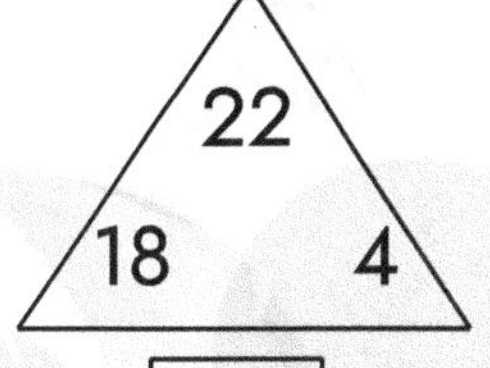

[ ] + [ ] = [ ]

[ ] + [ ] = [ ]

[ ] - [ ] = [ ]

[ ] - [ ] = [ ]

11.

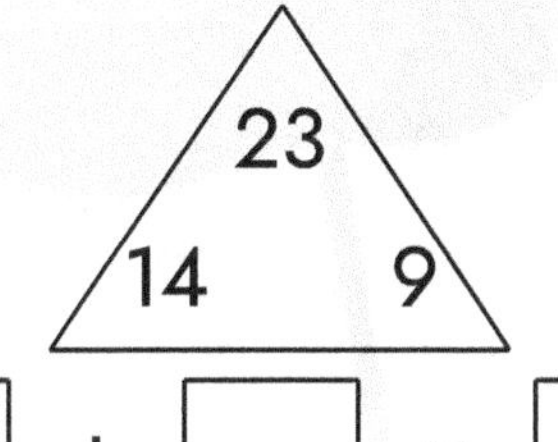

[ ] + [ ] = [ ]

[ ] + [ ] = [ ]

[ ] - [ ] = [ ]

[ ] - [ ] = [ ]

12.

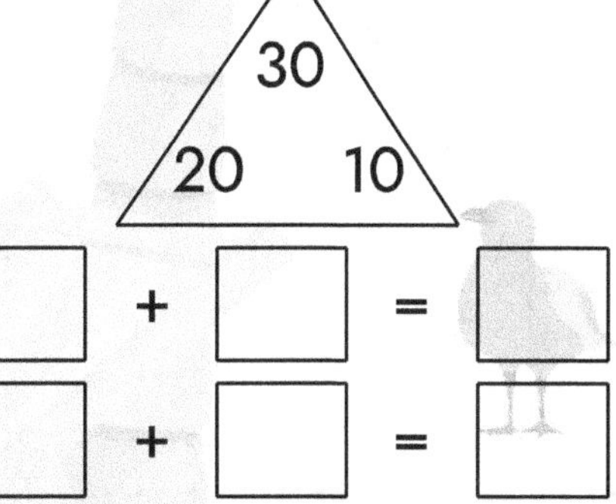

SUMMER MATH WORKBOOK
NAME:
BUILDING ACTIVITIES

32
17   15

22
18   4

23
14   9

30
20   10

[ ] + [ ] = [ ]

[ ] + [ ] = [ ]

[ ] - [ ] = [ ]

[ ] - [ ] = [ ]

13.

19
6   13

☐ + ☐ = ☐

☐ + ☐ = ☐

☐ - ☐ = ☐

☐ - ☐ = ☐

14.

15
5   10

☐ + ☐ = ☐

☐ + ☐ = ☐

☐ - ☐ = ☐

☐ - ☐ = ☐

15.

12
7   5

☐ + ☐ = ☐

☐ + ☐ = ☐

☐ - ☐ = ☐

☐ - ☐ = ☐

16.

23
20   3

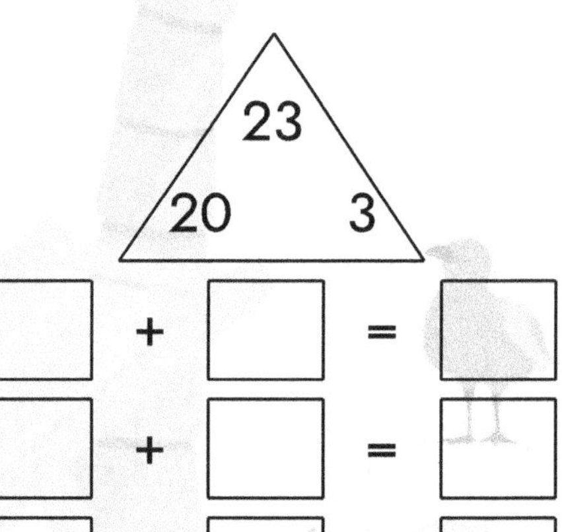

☐ + ☐ = ☐

☐ + ☐ = ☐

☐ - ☐ = ☐

☐ - ☐ = ☐

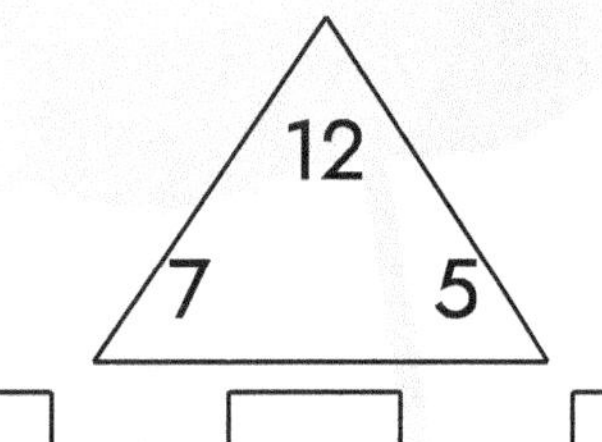
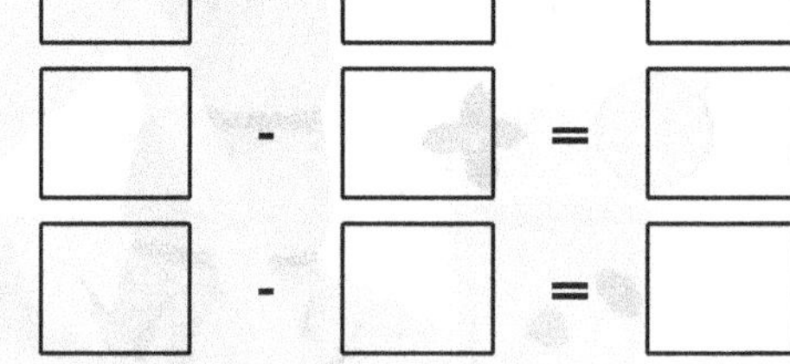

17.

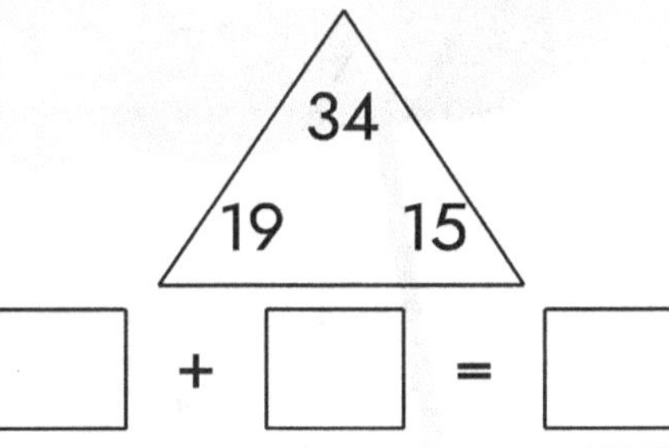

☐ + ☐ = ☐

☐ + ☐ = ☐

☐ - ☐ = ☐

☐ - ☐ = ☐

18.

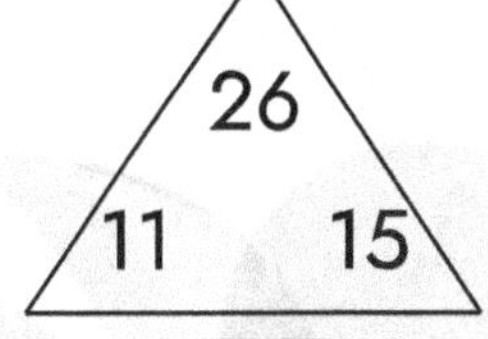

☐ + ☐ = ☐

☐ + ☐ = ☐

☐ - ☐ = ☐

☐ - ☐ = ☐

19.

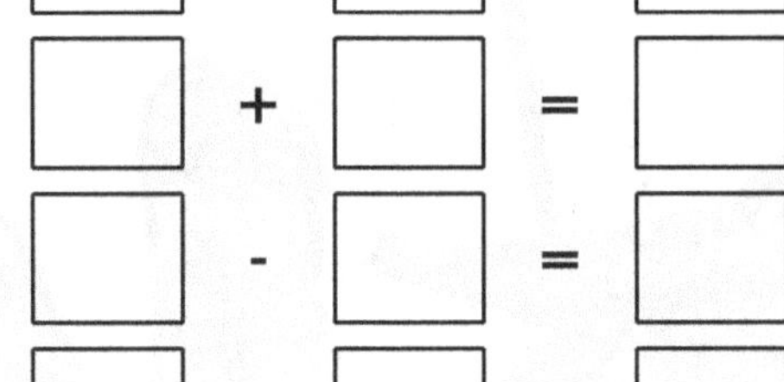

☐ + ☐ = ☐

☐ + ☐ = ☐

☐ - ☐ = ☐

☐ - ☐ = ☐

20.

☐ + ☐ = ☐

☐ + ☐ = ☐

☐ - ☐ = ☐

☐ - ☐ = ☐

21.

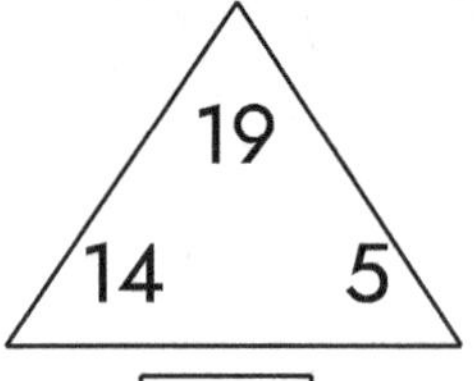

[ ] + [ ] = [ ]
[ ] + [ ] = [ ]
[ ] - [ ] = [ ]
[ ] - [ ] = [ ]

22.

12
9   3

[ ] + [ ] = [ ]
[ ] + [ ] = [ ]
[ ] - [ ] = [ ]
[ ] - [ ] = [ ]

23.

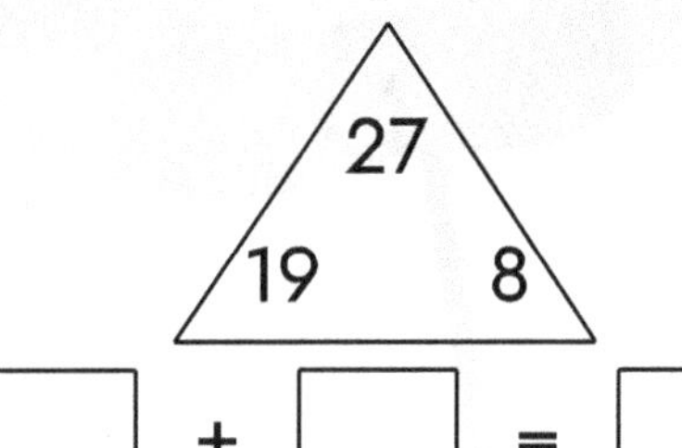

[ ] + [ ] = [ ]
[ ] + [ ] = [ ]
[ ] - [ ] = [ ]
[ ] - [ ] = [ ]

24.

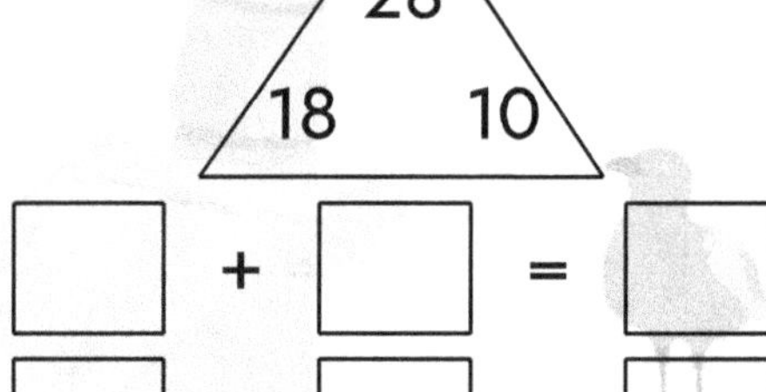

[ ] + [ ] = [ ]
[ ] + [ ] = [ ]
[ ] - [ ] = [ ]
[ ] - [ ] = [ ]

25.

23
3   20

☐ + ☐ = ☐
☐ + ☐ = ☐
☐ - ☐ = ☐
☐ - ☐ = ☐

26.

21
17   4

☐ + ☐ = ☐
☐ + ☐ = ☐
☐ - ☐ = ☐
☐ - ☐ = ☐

27.

15
12   3

☐ + ☐ = ☐
☐ + ☐ = ☐
☐ - ☐ = ☐
☐ - ☐ = ☐

28.

21
12   9

☐ + ☐ = ☐
☐ + ☐ = ☐
☐ - ☐ = ☐
☐ - ☐ = ☐

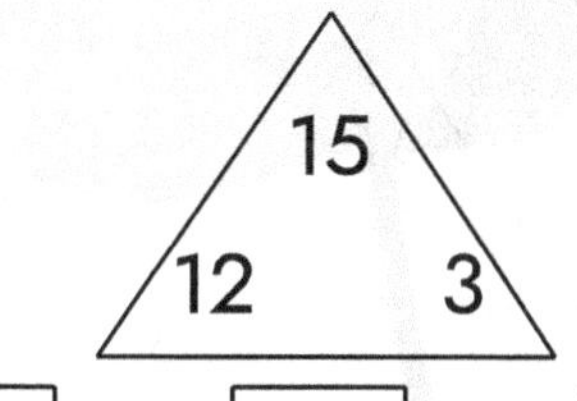
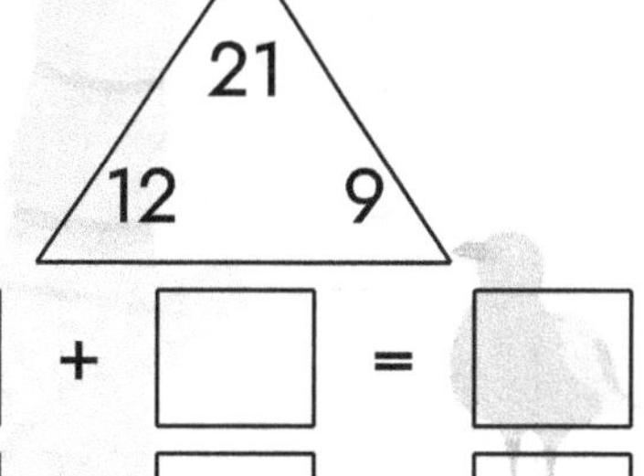

29.

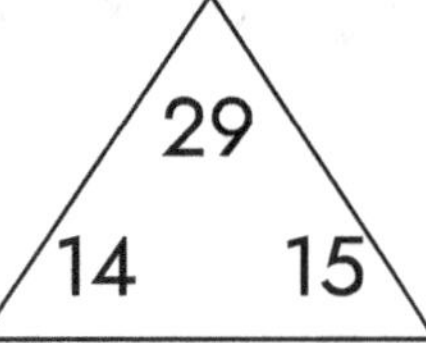

☐	+	☐	=	☐
☐	+	☐	=	☐
☐	−	☐	=	☐
☐	−	☐	=	☐

30.

☐	+	☐	=	☐
☐	+	☐	=	☐
☐	−	☐	=	☐
☐	−	☐	=	☐

31.

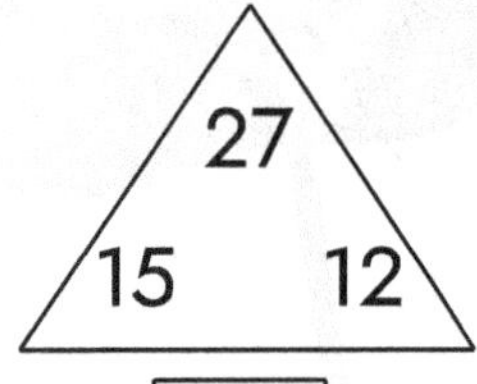

☐	+	☐	=	☐
☐	+	☐	=	☐
☐	−	☐	=	☐
☐	−	☐	=	☐

32.

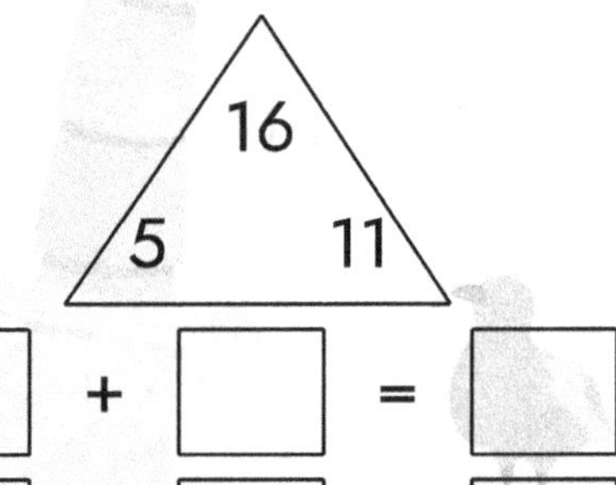

☐	+	☐	=	☐
☐	+	☐	=	☐
☐	−	☐	=	☐
☐	−	☐	=	☐

33.

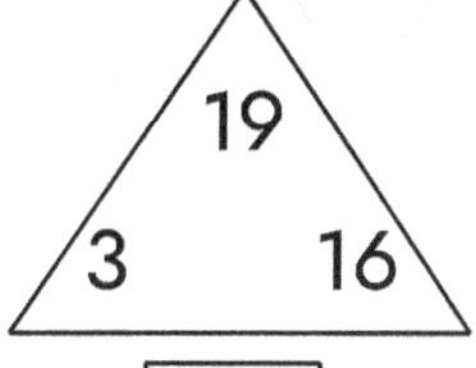

☐	+	☐	=	☐
☐	+	☐	=	☐
☐	-	☐	=	☐
☐	-	☐	=	☐

34.

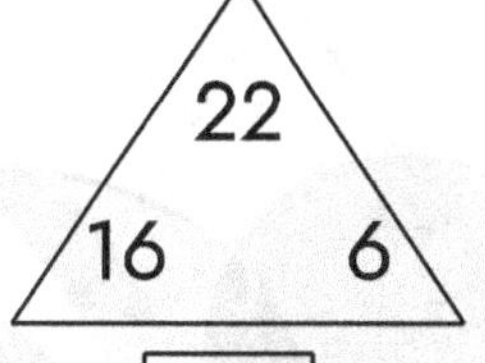

☐	+	☐	=	☐
☐	+	☐	=	☐
☐	-	☐	=	☐
☐	-	☐	=	☐

35.

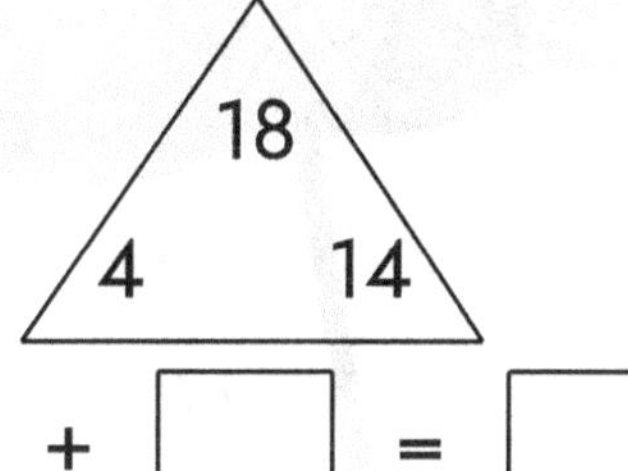

☐	+	☐	=	☐
☐	+	☐	=	☐
☐	-	☐	=	☐
☐	-	☐	=	☐

36.

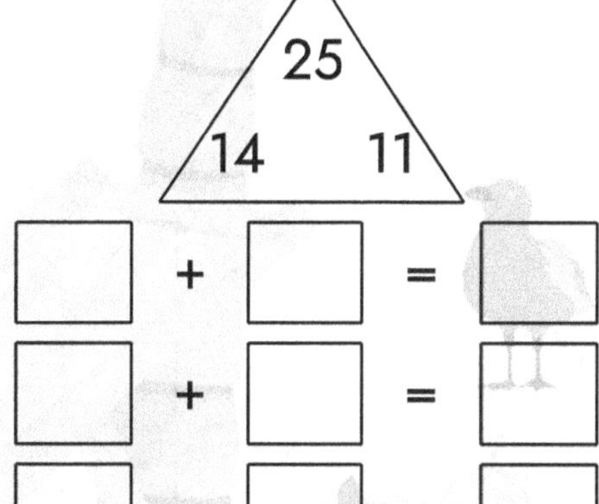

☐	+	☐	=	☐
☐	+	☐	=	☐
☐	-	☐	=	☐
☐	-	☐	=	☐

37.

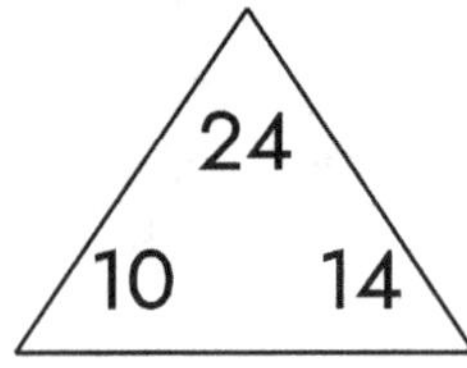

☐ + ☐ = ☐

☐ + ☐ = ☐

☐ - ☐ = ☐

☐ - ☐ = ☐

38.

☐ + ☐ = ☐

☐ + ☐ = ☐

☐ - ☐ = ☐

☐ - ☐ = ☐

39.

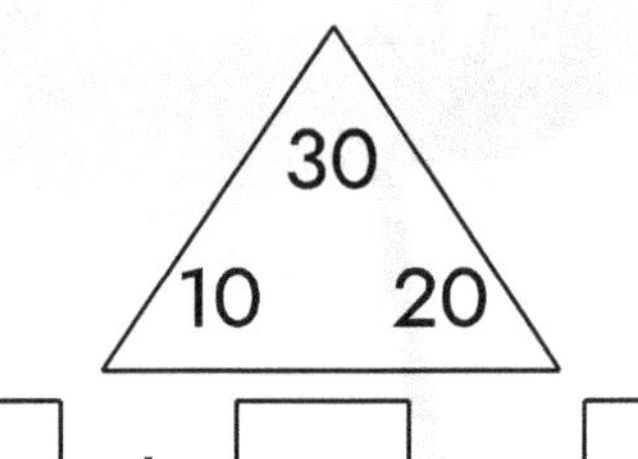

☐ + ☐ = ☐

☐ + ☐ = ☐

☐ - ☐ = ☐

☐ - ☐ = ☐

40.

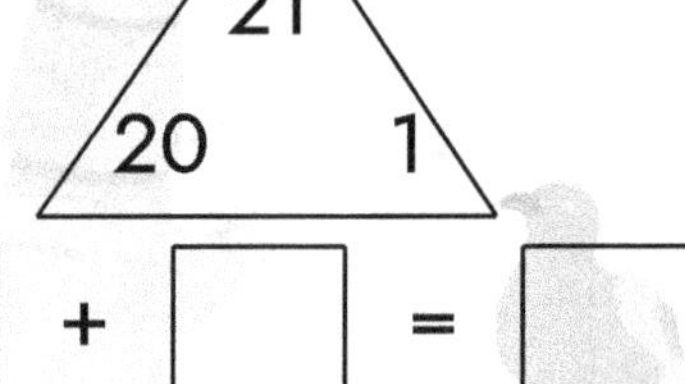

SUMMER MATH WORKBOOK
NAME:
BUILDING ACTIVITIES

24
10   14

5
1   4

30
10   20

21
20   1

☐ + ☐ = ☐

☐ + ☐ = ☐

☐ - ☐ = ☐

☐ - ☐ = ☐

Mixed Two-Digit Practice

Addition and Subtraction

1.	2.	3.	4.
93 − 66 —— 27	35 − 34 ——	42 + 12 ——	78 − 12 ——

5.	6.	7.	8.
20 − 17 ——	44 + 33 ——	31 + 44 ——	32 + 42 ——

9.	10.	11.	12.
31 + 37 ——	97 − 67 ——	27 + 11 ——	78 − 22 ——

13.	14.	15.	16.
39 − 19 ——	25 + 39 ——	12 + 18 ——	41 − 32 ——

17. $\begin{array}{r} 48 \\ + 11 \\ \hline \end{array}$	**18.** $\begin{array}{r} 26 \\ + 31 \\ \hline \end{array}$	**19.** $\begin{array}{r} 23 \\ - 18 \\ \hline \end{array}$	**20.** $\begin{array}{r} 30 \\ + 22 \\ \hline \end{array}$
21. $\begin{array}{r} 49 \\ + 15 \\ \hline \end{array}$	**22.** $\begin{array}{r} 37 \\ - 36 \\ \hline \end{array}$	**23.** $\begin{array}{r} 49 \\ - 35 \\ \hline \end{array}$	**24.** $\begin{array}{r} 29 \\ - 22 \\ \hline \end{array}$
25. $\begin{array}{r} 32 \\ + 45 \\ \hline \end{array}$	**26.** $\begin{array}{r} 29 \\ + 49 \\ \hline \end{array}$	**27.** $\begin{array}{r} 56 \\ - 42 \\ \hline \end{array}$	**28.** $\begin{array}{r} 38 \\ + 40 \\ \hline \end{array}$
29. $\begin{array}{r} 33 \\ + 19 \\ \hline \end{array}$	**30.** $\begin{array}{r} 48 \\ + 48 \\ \hline \end{array}$	**31.** $\begin{array}{r} 57 \\ - 21 \\ \hline \end{array}$	**32.** $\begin{array}{r} 42 \\ + 28 \\ \hline \end{array}$
33. $\begin{array}{r} 32 \\ - 32 \\ \hline \end{array}$	**34.** $\begin{array}{r} 22 \\ - 19 \\ \hline \end{array}$	**35.** $\begin{array}{r} 80 \\ - 57 \\ \hline \end{array}$	**36.** $\begin{array}{r} 60 \\ - 31 \\ \hline \end{array}$

37. 28 + 16	**38.** 20 + 38	**39.** 50 − 12	**40.** 32 + 32
41. 25 + 22	**42.** 43 + 34	**43.** 14 + 28	**44.** 44 + 50
45. 41 + 47	**46.** 29 + 41	**47.** 35 + 30	**48.** 89 − 38
49. 50 − 26	**50.** 13 + 39	**51.** 80 − 40	**52.** 49 − 46
53. 11 + 36	**54.** 25 + 33	**55.** 18 − 15	**56.** 34 − 10

57. $\begin{array}{r} 14 \\ +\ 40 \\ \hline \end{array}$	**58.** $\begin{array}{r} 13 \\ +\ 18 \\ \hline \end{array}$	**59.** $\begin{array}{r} 69 \\ -\ 22 \\ \hline \end{array}$	**60.** $\begin{array}{r} 47 \\ -\ 10 \\ \hline \end{array}$
61. $\begin{array}{r} 57 \\ -\ 24 \\ \hline \end{array}$	**62.** $\begin{array}{r} 50 \\ -\ 36 \\ \hline \end{array}$	**63.** $\begin{array}{r} 14 \\ +\ 26 \\ \hline \end{array}$	**64.** $\begin{array}{r} 50 \\ -\ 13 \\ \hline \end{array}$
65. $\begin{array}{r} 54 \\ -\ 49 \\ \hline \end{array}$	**66.** $\begin{array}{r} 50 \\ -\ 50 \\ \hline \end{array}$	**67.** $\begin{array}{r} 47 \\ +\ 35 \\ \hline \end{array}$	**68.** $\begin{array}{r} 40 \\ +\ 42 \\ \hline \end{array}$
69. $\begin{array}{r} 41 \\ +\ 39 \\ \hline \end{array}$	**70.** $\begin{array}{r} 57 \\ -\ 11 \\ \hline \end{array}$	**71.** $\begin{array}{r} 44 \\ -\ 32 \\ \hline \end{array}$	**72.** $\begin{array}{r} 76 \\ -\ 72 \\ \hline \end{array}$
73. $\begin{array}{r} 49 \\ +\ 48 \\ \hline \end{array}$	**74.** $\begin{array}{r} 34 \\ -\ 12 \\ \hline \end{array}$	**75.** $\begin{array}{r} 71 \\ -\ 68 \\ \hline \end{array}$	**76.** $\begin{array}{r} 85 \\ -\ 69 \\ \hline \end{array}$

Addition with Regrouping

Find the sum.

1.	27 + 83 — 110	**2.**	64 + 97	**3.**	97 + 36	**4.**	38 + 94
5.	41 + 89	**6.**	24 + 96	**7.**	96 + 85	**8.**	64 + 88
9.	87 + 69	**10.**	95 + 87	**11.**	91 + 49	**12.**	57 + 89
13.	87 + 39	**14.**	76 + 66	**15.**	55 + 58	**16.**	52 + 59

17. $\begin{array}{r} 51 \\ + 69 \\ \hline \end{array}$	**18.** $\begin{array}{r} 51 \\ + 89 \\ \hline \end{array}$	**19.** $\begin{array}{r} 91 \\ + 39 \\ \hline \end{array}$	**20.** $\begin{array}{r} 71 \\ + 69 \\ \hline \end{array}$
21. $\begin{array}{r} 54 \\ + 56 \\ \hline \end{array}$	**22.** $\begin{array}{r} 97 \\ + 54 \\ \hline \end{array}$	**23.** $\begin{array}{r} 52 \\ + 88 \\ \hline \end{array}$	**24.** $\begin{array}{r} 17 \\ + 95 \\ \hline \end{array}$
25. $\begin{array}{r} 16 \\ + 95 \\ \hline \end{array}$	**26.** $\begin{array}{r} 89 \\ + 79 \\ \hline \end{array}$	**27.** $\begin{array}{r} 15 \\ + 97 \\ \hline \end{array}$	**28.** $\begin{array}{r} 53 \\ + 79 \\ \hline \end{array}$
29. $\begin{array}{r} 49 \\ + 87 \\ \hline \end{array}$	**30.** $\begin{array}{r} 38 \\ + 89 \\ \hline \end{array}$	**31.** $\begin{array}{r} 83 \\ + 37 \\ \hline \end{array}$	**32.** $\begin{array}{r} 41 \\ + 79 \\ \hline \end{array}$
33. $\begin{array}{r} 44 \\ + 89 \\ \hline \end{array}$	**34.** $\begin{array}{r} 69 \\ + 75 \\ \hline \end{array}$	**35.** $\begin{array}{r} 21 \\ + 89 \\ \hline \end{array}$	**36.** $\begin{array}{r} 75 \\ + 98 \\ \hline \end{array}$

37. $94 + 49$	**38.** $41 + 99$	**39.** $19 + 97$	**40.** $44 + 96$
41. $47 + 95$	**42.** $79 + 75$	**43.** $81 + 39$	**44.** $57 + 83$
45. $77 + 93$	**46.** $23 + 88$	**47.** $36 + 84$	**48.** $69 + 71$
49. $53 + 87$	**50.** $36 + 96$	**51.** $94 + 66$	**52.** $14 + 98$
53. $31 + 89$	**54.** $36 + 98$	**55.** $67 + 83$	**56.** $31 + 99$

57.
57
+ 69
___

58.
97
+ 18
___

59.
77
+ 46
___

60.
97
+ 26
___

61.
26
+ 98
___

62.
74
+ 78
___

63.
23
+ 97
___

64.
24
+ 98
___

65.
51
+ 59
___

66.
66
+ 67
___

67.
97
+ 58
___

68.
63
+ 88
___

69.
23
+ 87
___

70.
76
+ 45
___

71.
15
+ 99
___

72.
42
+ 78
___

73.
45
+ 67
___

74.
54
+ 87
___

75.
94
+ 69
___

76.
15
+ 98
___

Subtraction with Regrouping

Find the difference.

1.
  76
− 69
————
  7

2.
  60
− 18
————

3.
  96
− 38
————

4.
  23
− 18
————

5.
  23
− 15
————

6.
  48
− 29
————

7.
  88
− 79
————

8.
  62
− 17
————

9.
  56
− 37
————

10.
  57
− 49
————

11.
  67
− 59
————

12.
  57
− 29
————

13.
  73
− 56
————

14.
  81
− 46
————

15.
  33
− 27
————

16.
  91
− 39
————

17. 53 − 17	18. 74 − 38	19. 94 − 46	20. 45 − 37
21. 42 − 15	22. 51 − 48	23. 88 − 59	24. 58 − 29
25. 63 − 35	26. 28 − 19	27. 65 − 57	28. 44 − 17
29. 50 − 21	30. 57 − 39	31. 27 − 18	32. 97 − 18
33. 95 − 89	34. 37 − 28	35. 33 − 16	36. 47 − 28

37. 82 − 26	**38.** 96 − 77	**39.** 42 − 24	**40.** 34 − 19
41. 58 − 49	**42.** 25 − 19	**43.** 98 − 19	**44.** 46 − 38
45. 27 − 19	**46.** 53 − 27	**47.** 25 − 18	**48.** 35 − 29
49. 20 − 14	**50.** 50 − 11	**51.** 40 − 33	**52.** 52 − 23
53. 60 − 31	**54.** 74 − 48	**55.** 81 − 69	**56.** 48 − 19

57.
$$\begin{array}{r} 22 \\ -\ 13 \\ \hline \end{array}$$

58.
$$\begin{array}{r} 25 \\ -\ 17 \\ \hline \end{array}$$

59.
$$\begin{array}{r} 82 \\ -\ 66 \\ \hline \end{array}$$

60.
$$\begin{array}{r} 76 \\ -\ 47 \\ \hline \end{array}$$

61.
$$\begin{array}{r} 34 \\ -\ 26 \\ \hline \end{array}$$

62.
$$\begin{array}{r} 21 \\ -\ 12 \\ \hline \end{array}$$

63.
$$\begin{array}{r} 47 \\ -\ 18 \\ \hline \end{array}$$

64.
$$\begin{array}{r} 44 \\ -\ 27 \\ \hline \end{array}$$

65.
$$\begin{array}{r} 68 \\ -\ 59 \\ \hline \end{array}$$

66.
$$\begin{array}{r} 40 \\ -\ 34 \\ \hline \end{array}$$

67.
$$\begin{array}{r} 60 \\ -\ 43 \\ \hline \end{array}$$

68.
$$\begin{array}{r} 63 \\ -\ 18 \\ \hline \end{array}$$

69.
$$\begin{array}{r} 64 \\ -\ 25 \\ \hline \end{array}$$

70.
$$\begin{array}{r} 36 \\ -\ 28 \\ \hline \end{array}$$

71.
$$\begin{array}{r} 46 \\ -\ 17 \\ \hline \end{array}$$

72.
$$\begin{array}{r} 41 \\ -\ 27 \\ \hline \end{array}$$

73.
$$\begin{array}{r} 86 \\ -\ 77 \\ \hline \end{array}$$

74.
$$\begin{array}{r} 86 \\ -\ 69 \\ \hline \end{array}$$

75.
$$\begin{array}{r} 70 \\ -\ 63 \\ \hline \end{array}$$

76.
$$\begin{array}{r} 80 \\ -\ 77 \\ \hline \end{array}$$

Can you Make 100?

Find the numbers.

1. 36 + 64 = 100

2. 16 + ___ = 100

3. 4 + ___ = 100

4. 31 + ___ = 100

5. 18 + ___ = 100

6. 9 + ___ = 100

7. 21 + ___ = 100

8. 27 + ___ = 100

9. 37 + ___ = 100

10. 11 + ___ = 100

11. 5 + ___ = 100

12. 22 + ___ = 100

13. 34 + ___ = 100

14. 14 + ___ = 100

15. 29 + ___ = 100

16. 28 + ___ = 100

17. 10 + ___ = 100

18. 26 + ___ = 100

19. 6 + ___ = 100

20. 15 + ___ = 100

21. 8 + ___ = 100

22. 3 + ___ = 100

23. 35 + ___ = 100

24. 13 + ___ = 100

25. 23 + ___ = 100

26. 33 + ___ = 100

27. 17 + ___ = 100

28. 12 + ___ = 100

29. 7 + ___ = 100

30. 39 + ___ = 100

31. 30 + ___ = 100

32. 25 + ___ = 100

33. 24 + ___ = 100

34. 2 + ___ = 100

35. 1 + ___ = 100

36. 20 + ___ = 100

Place Value

Determine the place value of the underlined digit.

1. 6<u>3</u>1 = _3 tens_

2. 4<u>7</u>7 = _____________

3. 71<u>3</u> = _____________

4. 7<u>9</u>8 = _____________

5. 4<u>3</u>9 = _____________

6. 74<u>9</u> = _____________

7. <u>3</u>71 = _____________

8. 9<u>4</u>8 = _____________

9. <u>5</u>98 = _____________

10. 7<u>0</u>2 = _____________

11. 2<u>8</u>3 = _____________

12. <u>1</u>80 = _____________

13. 71<u>2</u> = _____________

14. 46<u>8</u> = _____________

15. 3<u>4</u>5 = _____________

16. <u>2</u>79 = _____________

17. 7<u>3</u> = _________________

18. 30<u>4</u> = _________________

19. 1<u>4</u>3 = _________________

20. 84<u>1</u> = _________________

21. 9<u>7</u>1 = _________________

22. <u>8</u>95 = _________________

23. 3<u>1</u>8 = _________________

24. <u>8</u>56 = _________________

25. <u>3</u>28 = _________________

26. <u>2</u>43 = _________________

27. 2<u>1</u>5 = _________________

28. 61<u>3</u> = _________________

29. 95<u>4</u> = _________________

30. 28<u>9</u> = _________________

31. 1<u>1</u>2 = _________________

32. 6<u>7</u>1 = _________________

33. <u>6</u>52 = _________________

34. 5<u>4</u>2 = _________________

35. 4<u>7</u>0 = _______________

36. 8<u>8</u>5 = _______________

37. 18<u>2</u> = _______________

38. <u>5</u>88 = _______________

39. 73<u>1</u> = _______________

40. 29<u>3</u> = _______________

41. 1<u>2</u>0 = _______________

42. 44<u>8</u> = _______________

43. <u>8</u>63 = _______________

44. <u>9</u>81 = _______________

45. 2<u>7</u>0 = _______________

46. <u>8</u>88 = _______________

47. 9<u>0</u>1 = _______________

48. 2<u>9</u> = _______________

49. 19<u>4</u> = _______________

50. <u>1</u>83 = _______________

51. <u>8</u>70 = _______________

52. 6<u>5</u> = _______________

53. 5_2_4 = _______________

54. _7_36 = _______________

55. _1_60 = _______________

56. _4_71 = _______________

57. _1_97 = _______________

58. 53_5_ = _______________

59. _7_58 = _______________

60. _9_94 = _______________

61. 3_1_0 = _______________

62. _5_91 = _______________

63. 6_1_2 = _______________

64. 5_2_8 = _______________

65. _1_71 = _______________

66. _9_97 = _______________

67. 46_0_ = _______________

68. 9_3_3 = _______________

69. 8_9_1 = _______________

70. _7_16 = _______________

Place Value: Expanded Notation

Provide the expanded notation for each value.

1. _348_ three hundred forty-eight

2. _________ four hundred forty-six

3. _________ twenty-one

4. _________ five hundred eight

5. _________ two hundred ninety-eight

6. _________ five hundred fifty-one

7. _________ nine hundred seventy-five

8. _________ three hundred sixty-three

9. _________ six hundred forty-eight

10. _________ nine hundred twenty-four

11. _________ six hundred thirteen

12. _________ five hundred sixty

13. _________ eight hundred three

14. _________ five hundred sixty-six

15. _________ six hundred forty-one

16. _________ eight hundred thirty-five

17. _________ sixty-two

18. _________ one hundred twenty-three

19. _________ one hundred forty-four

20. _________ two hundred forty-three

21. _________ five hundred three

22. _________ nine hundred forty-five

23. _________ nine hundred eighty

24. _________ five hundred twenty-four

25. _________ four hundred seventy-seven

26. _________ ninety-eight

27. _________ two hundred five

28. _________ eight hundred eleven

29. _________ one hundred fifty-eight

30. _________ four hundred sixty-eight

31. _________ four hundred twenty-three

32. _________ one hundred ninety-eight

33. _________ four hundred sixty-nine

34. _________ eight hundred sixty-seven

35. _________ eight hundred four

36. _________ eight hundred eighteen

37. _________ seven hundred fourteen

38. _________ nine hundred thirty-eight

39. _________ eight hundred eighty-three

40. _________ seven hundred seventy-three

41. _________ two hundred forty-two

42. _________ six hundred fifty-two

43. _________ eighty

44. _________ three hundred eighty-six

45. _________ five hundred sixty-nine

46. _________ nine hundred forty-six

47. _________ five hundred fourteen

48. _________ seventy-two

49. _________ seven hundred seventy-one

50. _________ one hundred eighty-two

51. _________ nine hundred fifty

52. _________ six hundred seventy-one

53. _________ three hundred twenty

54. _________ one hundred one

55. _________ five hundred seventy

56. _________ four hundred three

57. _________ four hundred sixty-six

58. _________ four hundred ninety-seven

59. _________ thirty-one

60. _________ two hundred one

61. __________ one hundred sixty-five

62. __________ two hundred six

63. __________ one hundred eighty-one

64. __________ five hundred two

65. __________ four hundred fifteen

66. __________ ninety-two

67. __________ nine hundred thirty-five

68. __________ seven hundred sixty-two

69. __________ eight hundred twenty-three

70. __________ one hundred twenty-two

71. __________ one hundred twenty-four

72. __________ two hundred forty

73. _________ three hundred seventy-one

74. _________ three

75. _________ eight hundred fifty-one

76. _________ eight hundred sixty-five

77. _________ five hundred ninety-five

78. _________ nine hundred fifty-five

79. _________ five hundred thirty-two

80. _________ five hundred eighty-four

81. _________ one hundred thirty-three

82. _________ forty-one

83. _________ nine hundred seventy-six

84. _________ five hundred eighteen

85. __________ seven hundred fifty-two

86. __________ eight hundred seventy-eight

87. __________ three hundred sixty-nine

88. __________ four hundred two

89. __________ three hundred fifty-three

90. __________ two hundred eighteen

91. __________ nine hundred seven

92. __________ six hundred eighty-three

93. __________ four hundred twenty-six

94. __________ seventy-eight

95. __________ four hundred forty-seven

96. __________ nine hundred

Addition Quiz

1. 17 + 20 = ___

    A. 34

    B. 39

    C. 36

    D. 37

2. 5 + 16 = ___

    A. 16

    B. 21

    C. 22

    D. 18

3. 13 + 20 = ___

    A. 32

    B. 33

    C. 34

    D. 36

4. 2 + 12 = ___

    A. 18

    B. 19

    C. 14

    D. 16

5. 8 + 19 = ___

    A. 27

    B. 23

    C. 29

    D. 22

6. 6 + 9 = ___

    A. 13

    B. 15

    C. 14

    D. 19

7. 19 + 19 = ___
    A. 40
    B. 38
    C. 34
    D. 35

10. 13 + 11 = ___
    A. 28
    B. 26
    C. 29
    D. 24

8. 13 + 20 = ___
    A. 37
    B. 30
    C. 35
    D. 33

11. 12 + 3 = ___
    A. 10
    B. 17
    C. 15
    D. 16

9. 19 + 1 = ___
    A. 24
    B. 25
    C. 19
    D. 20

12. 20 + 14 = ___
    A. 34
    B. 32
    C. 35
    D. 39

13. 20 + 9 = ____
    A. 32
    B. 25
    C. 29
    D. 33

16. 14 + 10 = ____
    A. 24
    B. 22
    C. 23
    D. 29

14. 20 + 12 = ____
    A. 37
    B. 32
    C. 31
    D. 33

17. 9 + 18 = ____
    A. 22
    B. 27
    C. 31
    D. 25

15. 3 + 4 = ____
    A. 7
    B. 12
    C. 8
    D. 5

18. 1 + 14 = ____
    A. 15
    B. 19
    C. 13
    D. 14

19. 3 + 2 = ___
A. 8
B. 5
C. 4
D. 3

22. 17 + 9 = ___
A. 26
B. 29
C. 21
D. 25

20. 13 + 16 = ___
A. 31
B. 25
C. 28
D. 29

23. 8 + 3 = ___
A. 14
B. 11
C. 6
D. 7

21. 13 + 19 = ___
A. 28
B. 29
C. 31
D. 32

24. 12 + 6 = ___
A. 18
B. 23
C. 21
D. 16

SUMMER MATH WORKBOOK

BUILDING ACTIVITIES

Subtraction Quiz

1. 18 - 8 = ___
   - A. 10
   - B. -8
   - C. 11
   - D. -6

2. 5 - 4 = ___
   - A. 1
   - B. -12
   - C. -2
   - D. 8

3. 17 - 9 = ___
   - A. -5
   - B. -7
   - C. -1
   - D. 8

4. 13 - 10 = ___
   - A. 10
   - B. -6
   - C. 18
   - D. 3

5. 5 - 6 = ___
   - A. -10
   - B. 15
   - C. 2
   - D. -1

6. 5 - 7 = ___
   - A. -7
   - B. -20
   - C. -13
   - D. -2

7. 16 - 1 = ___

    A. 12

    B. 15

    C. 11

    D. 30

8. 6 - 7 = ___

    A. -5

    B. -1

    C. 15

    D. 14

9. 15 - 12 = ___

    A. 11

    B. 12

    C. 3

    D. 4

10. 2 - 5 = ___

    A. 16

    B. -3

    C. -19

    D. -6

11. 10 - 13 = ___

    A. -3

    B. 16

    C. -2

    D. 2

12. 2 - 9 = ___

    A. 7

    B. 13

    C. -7

    D. -25

13. 6 - 16 = ___
   A. 8
   B. -26
   C. -15
   D. -10

14. 2 - 3 = ___
   A. -16
   B. -1
   C. 8
   D. 4

15. 20 - 14 = ___
   A. 6
   B. 17
   C. 19
   D. -8

16. 15 - 1 = ___
   A. 14
   B. 0
   C. -3
   D. 33

17. 17 - 11 = ___
   A. 17
   B. -13
   C. 20
   D. 6

18. 12 - 13 = ___
   A. -1
   B. 18
   C. -5
   D. 19

19. 4 - 1 = ___

A. 8

B. 3

C. 13

D. 0

20. 10 - 7 = ___

A. -5

B. -3

C. 3

D. -2

21. 20 - 7 = ___

A. 13

B. 21

C. 18

D. 11

22. 10 - 9 = ___

A. -1

B. 1

C. -18

D. 11

23. 7 - 1 = ___

A. -2

B. 11

C. -4

D. 6

24. 15 - 7 = ___

A. 8

B. 10

C. -8

D. -10

ANSWERS

Page 1: Counting Up and Down

1. | 546 | 547 | 548 | 549 | 550 |

2. | 754 | 755 | 756 | 757 | 758 |

3. | 44 | 45 | 46 | 47 | 48 |

4. | 78 | 77 | 76 | 75 | 74 |

5. | 745 | 746 | 747 | 748 | 749 |

6. | 17 | 18 | 19 | 20 | 21 |

7. | 823 | 822 | 821 | 820 | 819 |

8. | 154 | 153 | 152 | 151 | 150 |

9. | 739 | 738 | 737 | 736 | 735 |

10. | 356 | 357 | 358 | 359 | 360 |

11. | 559 | 560 | 561 | 562 | 563 |

12. | 283 | 282 | 281 | 280 | 279 |

13. | 782 | 781 | 780 | 779 | 778 |

14. | 298 | 297 | 296 | 295 | 294 |

15. | 182 | 183 | 184 | 185 | 186 |

16. | 803 | 804 | 805 | 806 | 807 |

17. | 603 | 602 | 601 | 600 | 599 |

18. | 939 | 938 | 937 | 936 | 935 |

19. | 404 | 403 | 402 | 401 | 400 |

20. | 664 | 663 | 662 | 661 | 660 |

21.

| 307 | 308 | 309 | 310 | 311 |

22.

| 661 | 662 | 663 | 664 | 665 |

23.

| 811 | 812 | 813 | 814 | 815 |

24.

| 513 | 514 | 515 | 516 | 517 |

25.

| 104 | 103 | 102 | 101 | 100 |

26.

| 441 | 442 | 443 | 444 | 445 |

Page 3:   Counting Patterns: Count by 2s to 5s

1.

| 427 | 429 | 431 | 433 | 435 |

2.

| 600 | 602 | 604 | 606 | 608 |

3.

| 191 | 195 | 199 | 203 | 207 |

4.

| 316 | 318 | 320 | 322 | 324 |

5.

| 596 | 598 | 600 | 602 | 604 |

6.

| 933 | 935 | 937 | 939 | 941 |

7.

| 300 | 303 | 306 | 309 | 312 |

8.

| 315 | 318 | 321 | 324 | 327 |

9.

| 751 | 753 | 755 | 757 | 759 |

10.

| 573 | 577 | 581 | 585 | 589 |

11.

| 733 | 738 | 743 | 748 | 753 |

12.

| 882 | 884 | 886 | 888 | 890 |

13.

| 171 | 173 | 175 | 177 | 179 |

14.

| 886 | 888 | 890 | 892 | 894 |

15.

| 468 | 472 | 476 | 480 | 484 |

16.

| 919 | 923 | 927 | 931 | 935 |

17.

952	957	962	967	972

18.

320	325	330	335	340

19.

201	205	209	213	217

20.

335	337	339	341	343

21.

636	639	642	645	648

22.

707	711	715	719	723

23.

547	550	553	556	559

24.

799	802	805	808	811

25.

776	780	784	788	792

26.

880	883	886	889	892

27.

815	818	821	824	827

28.

292	296	300	304	308

Page 6:   Comparing the Numbers

1. <   2. <   3. >   4. <   5. <   6. >   7. >   8. <   9. <   10. >

11. <   12. <   13. <   14. >   15. >   16. >   17. <   18. >   19. <   20. <

21. >   22. <   23. >   24. >   25. >   26. <   27. >   28. <   29. >   30. <

31. <   32. <   33. <   34. >   35. >   36. >   37. <   38. >   39. <   40. >

41. <   42. >   43. >   44. >   45. <   46. <   47. >   48. <   49. <   50. >

51. >   52. >

Page 9:   Circle the Numbers

1. 564   461   (252)   274

2. 915   (277)   301   641

3. 414   989   (51)   398

4. (10)   392   275   840

5. (499) 623 589 732

6. 694 646 (415) 758

7. 895 772 (518) 799

8. 685 372 968 (100)

9. 592 660 600 (263)

10. 759 (22) 369 543

11. (256) 882 650 527

12. (34) 156 401 327

13. 635 551 (126) 368

14. 252 971 (174) 917

15. (47) 494 378 143

16. 759 501 956 (42)

17. (21) 950 805 349

18. 792 (12) 82 477

19. 254 (47) 477 811

20. 996 888 (725) 740

21. 372 191 165 (134)

22. (247) 600 847 621

23. 486 682 (217) 265

24. 643 (227) 783 755

25. 926 608 506 (83)

26. 350 (52) 534 623

27. 470 648 (114) 206

28. 494 363 921 (159)

29. 769 638 771 (568)

30. (337) 823 795 420

31. (103) 184 862 110

32. 795 816 833 (28)

Page 11: Circle the Numbers

1. 264 722 (885) 388

2. 382 (642) 390 320

3. 657 541 (663) 599

4. 486 (642) 127 124

5. (760) 59 496 6

6. (455) 215 418 104

7. 813 86 (979) 166

8. 189 425 (828) 654

9. 814 87 (941) 772

10. 477 534 (776) 127

11. 248 451 (911) 796

12. 160 197 (934) 461

13. 58 (739) 349 737

14. 320 (828) 572 49

15. 304 (781) 574 297

16. (662) 224 132 233

17. 712 10 (784) 400

18. (701) 355 646 227

19. 282 370 (758) 5

20. 304 622 (943) 617

21. 152 (519) 109 450

22. 76 92 334 (986)

23. 514 (892) 468 695

24. (959) 480 465 24

25. 320 (679) 84 151

26. 412 534 (759) 702

27. 93 123 455 (950)

28. 70 568 (745) 681

29. 838 (957) 145 143

30. 116 (681) 157 621

31. 675 798 (886) 808

32. 886 (950) 267 802

Page 13:   Circle the Numbers

1. (904) 734 685 (625)
2. 539 (793) (205) 618
3. 759 407 (357) (952)
4. 636 (384) 916 (946)
5. 148 786 (857) (2)
6. 335 (322) (908) 638
7. 522 (462) 475 (614)
8. 647 (951) 815 (143)
9. (855) 652 (46) 336
10. (882) 121 143 (45)
11. (753) 527 (383) 709
12. 325 (205) (984) 291
13. 881 (940) 660 (100)
14. (93) 266 468 (583)
15. (826) (47) 103 77
16. (318) 590 (970) 808
17. 591 215 (98) (984)
18. 339 (580) 64 (28)
19. 644 (812) (249) 808
20. (939) (200) 314 318
21. 478 (185) (732) 707
22. 291 (715) (50) 590
23. (185) 463 510 (835)
24. (18) 67 (727) 163
25. 556 (575) 118 (110)
26. 108 (1) (952) 301
27. (876) 633 456 (281)
28. (17) (660) 643 626
29. 733 (785) 598 (133)
30. 858 (263) 517 (875)

31. (165) 507 799 (876)

32. 71 229 (11) (578)

Page 15: Circle the Numbers

1. 86 252 364 82

2. 204 (211) 478 (233)

3. (431) (831) 658 260

4. (769) (573) (525) (819)

5. (883) (103) 232 468

6. 594 (305) (293) 58

7. (243) (945) 600 (201)

8. 76 (231) 648 (623)

9. 878 196 930 408

10. 280 544 (529) (575)

11. (121) 900 (427) 432

12. (859) (615) 396 (933)

13. (275) (57) (187) (127)

14. 778 110 (491) (781)

15. 958 (307) (839) (259)

16. 610 (277) (157) (201)

17. 184 (35) 382 574

18. 642 (117) 540 (339)

19. (573) 656 (347) 694

20. (877) (861) 198 (627)

21. (549) (667) (925) (19)

22. (45) (521) 844 768

23. 704 150 450 972

24. (705) (271) (965) 844

25. (743) (227) (249) (825)

26. 234 822 (291) (159)

27. (517) (847) (553) (123)

28. (763) (797) 904 (97)

29. 110 212 (709) (943)

30. (351) 138 (157) 662

31. (191) (613) (869) (493)

32. 666 (567) 634 302

Page 17: Circle the Numbers

1. 691 503 (950) (650)

2. 613 373 393 727

3. (376) 767 (502) 197

4. 967 (722) (6) 907

5. 245 353 863 493

6. (562) 23 493 (606)

7. 71 (586) (634) (620)

8. (952) 797 (492) (950)

9. (214) (252) 431 (260)

10. (846) (254) (484) (736)

11. (818) 981 567 (584)

12. (636) 959 (694) 469

13. (608) 961 249 (314)

14. (704) 141 (740) 669

15. (10) 345 (580) 27

16. (738) 773 (774) (578)

17. (276) (552) 983 (716)

18. 291 745 61 (990)

19. 869 127 675 (580)

20. 455 909 969 (112)

21. 891 (166) 13 (990)

22. 549 179 247 73

23. (512) (762) (250) (502)

24. (674) 457 (998) (46)

25. 207 (988) (308) 85

26. (976) (978) 179 (862)

27. 901 (258) (444) 577

28. (466) (160) (214) 101

29. 375 (468) 135 (572)

30. (760) 783 (30) 97

31. (306) (910) 205 (528)

32. 495 559 317 (412)

Page 23: Missing Numbers: Between

1. 129 **2.** 374 **3.** 602 **4.** 136 **5.** 988 **6.** 91 **7.** 735 **8.** 608

9. 550 **10.** 128 **11.** 323 **12.** 287 **13.** 960 **14.** 780 **15.** 774 **16.** 369

17. 942 **18.** 450 **19.** 788 **20.** 501 **21.** 334 **22.** 586 **23.** 694 **24.** 364

25. 305 **26.** 980 **27.** 433 **28.** 344 **29.** 508 **30.** 107 **31.** 142 **32.** 783

33. 351 **34.** 221 **35.** 566 **36.** 650 **37.** 873 **38.** 842 **39.** 731

Page 19: Missing Numbers: Before and After

1. 849 851 **2.** 761 763 **3.** 671 673 **4.** 909 911 **5.** 942 944

6. 494 496 **7.** 241 243 **8.** 384 386 **9.** 81 83 **10.** 828 830

11. 389 391 **12.** 416 418 **13.** 288 290 **14.** 696 698 **15.** 238 240

16. 860 862 **17.** 220 222 **18.** 540 542 **19.** 308 310 **20.** 666 668

21. 838 840 **22.** 760 762 **23.** 276 278 **24.** 560 562 **25.** 253 255

26. 20 22 **27.** 847 849 **28.** 832 834 **29.** 727 729 **30.** 633 635

31. 326 328 **32.** 593 595 **33.** 886 888 **34.** 618 620 **35.** 570 572

36. 955 957 **37.** 581 583 **38.** 108 110 **39.** 900 902

Page 24: Addition 1 to 20

1. 18 **2.** 17 **3.** 24 **4.** 25 **5.** 26 **6.** 18 **7.** 8 **8.** 16 **9.** 24

10. 35 **11.** 22 **12.** 16 **13.** 36 **14.** 17 **15.** 33 **16.** 22 **17.** 21 **18.** 22

19. 31 **20.** 33 **21.** 5 **22.** 15 **23.** 23 **24.** 15 **25.** 21 **26.** 22 **27.** 24

28. 11 **29.** 20 **30.** 36 **31.** 8 **32.** 25 **33.** 12 **34.** 14 **35.** 13 **36.** 23

37. 36 **38.** 28 **39.** 18 **40.** 29 **41.** 30 **42.** 11 **43.** 6 **44.** 13 **45.** 30

46. 37 **47.** 24 **48.** 27 **49.** 10 **50.** 19

Page 26: Double Digit Addition

1. 156 **2.** 63 **3.** 128 **4.** 79 **5.** 99 **6.** 140 **7.** 44 **8.** 160

9. 141 **10.** 139 **11.** 107 **12.** 139 **13.** 71 **14.** 164 **15.** 117 **16.** 74

17. 154 **18.** 32 **19.** 134 **20.** 29 **21.** 106 **22.** 99 **23.** 154 **24.** 162

25. 105 **26.** 111 **27.** 93 **28.** 155 **29.** 157 **30.** 110 **31.** 76 **32.** 169

33. 94 **34.** 108 **35.** 107 **36.** 44 **37.** 95 **38.** 192 **39.** 105 **40.** 129

41. 81 **42.** 135 **43.** 105 **44.** 97 **45.** 57 **46.** 116 **47.** 94 **48.** 49

49. 124 **50.** 40

Page 28: Subtraction 1 to 20

1. 5 **2.** 7 **3.** 0 **4.** 10 **5.** 2 **6.** 11 **7.** 3 **8.** 1 **9.** 0

10. 5 **11.** 2 **12.** 1 **13.** 7 **14.** 6 **15.** 3 **16.** 11 **17.** 9 **18.** 0

19. 3 **20.** 10 **21.** 9 **22.** 9 **23.** 8 **24.** 11 **25.** 1 **26.** 14 **27.** 13

28. 4 **29.** 11 **30.** 1 **31.** 4 **32.** 11 **33.** 2 **34.** 6 **35.** 5 **36.** 12

37. 8 **38.** 6 **39.** 13 **40.** 0 **41.** 1 **42.** 5 **43.** 11 **44.** 8 **45.** 4

Page 30: Double Digit Subtraction

1. 3 **2.** 14 **3.** 42 **4.** 7 **5.** 40 **6.** 9 **7.** 24 **8.** 36 **9.** 6

10. 43 **11.** 22 **12.** 24 **13.** 10 **14.** 2 **15.** 57 **16.** 65 **17.** 3 **18.** 1

19. 8 **20.** 31 **21.** 4 **22.** 2 **23.** 31 **24.** 30 **25.** 55 **26.** 1 **27.** 17

28. 11	**29.** 27	**30.** 36	**31.** 19	**32.** 13	**33.** 1	**34.** 3	**35.** 31	**36.** 6
37. 5	**38.** 10	**39.** 9	**40.** 17	**41.** 23	**42.** 30	**43.** 21	**44.** 11	**45.** 33
46. 16	**47.** 6	**48.** 2	**49.** 7	**50.** 17	**51.** 39	**52.** 25	**53.** 9	**54.** 46
55. 42	**56.** 28	**57.** 6	**58.** 17	**59.** 16	**60.** 74	**61.** 20	**62.** 79	**63.** 30
64. 5	**65.** 8	**66.** 8	**67.** 5	**68.** 3	**69.** 59	**70.** 11	**71.** 19	**72.** 12
73. 62	**74.** 34	**75.** 15	**76.** 1	**77.** 31	**78.** 1	**79.** 2	**80.** 1	**81.** 16
82. 0	**83.** 0	**84.** 23	**85.** 52	**86.** 14	**87.** 4	**88.** 49	**89.** 4	**90.** 39
91. 4	**92.** 1	**93.** 9	**94.** 41	**95.** 7				

Page 34: Addition - Doubles

1. 108	**2.** 92	**3.** 40	**4.** 160	**5.** 168	**6.** 38	**7.** 24	**8.** 148
9. 106	**10.** 132	**11.** 34	**12.** 20	**13.** 118	**14.** 86	**15.** 124	**16.** 188
17. 152	**18.** 94	**19.** 170	**20.** 66	**21.** 150	**22.** 26	**23.** 96	**24.** 52
25. 182	**26.** 98	**27.** 46	**28.** 192	**29.** 142	**30.** 110	**31.** 72	**32.** 90
33. 122	**34.** 154	**35.** 136	**36.** 102	**37.** 62	**38.** 156	**39.** 22	**40.** 166
41. 82	**42.** 174	**43.** 74	**44.** 100	**45.** 130	**46.** 172	**47.** 32	**48.** 178
49. 140	**50.** 190	**51.** 36	**52.** 48	**53.** 42	**54.** 56	**55.** 186	**56.** 30

Page 37:   Fact Families: Addition and Subtraction

1.
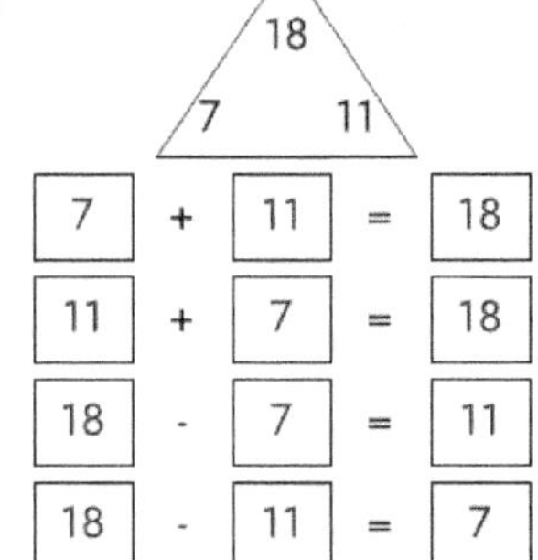

7	+	11	=	18
11	+	7	=	18
18	-	7	=	11
18	-	11	=	7

2.
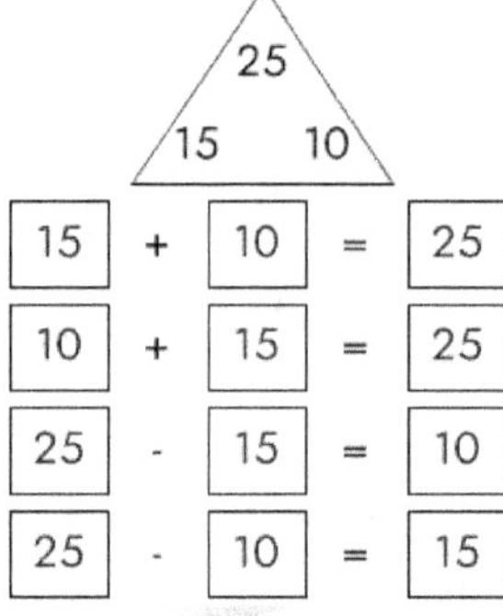

15	+	10	=	25
10	+	15	=	25
25	-	15	=	10
25	-	10	=	15

3.
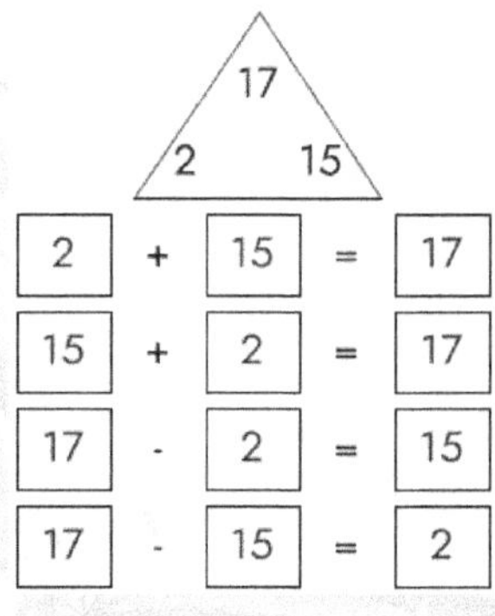

2	+	15	=	17
15	+	2	=	17
17	-	2	=	15
17	-	15	=	2

4.
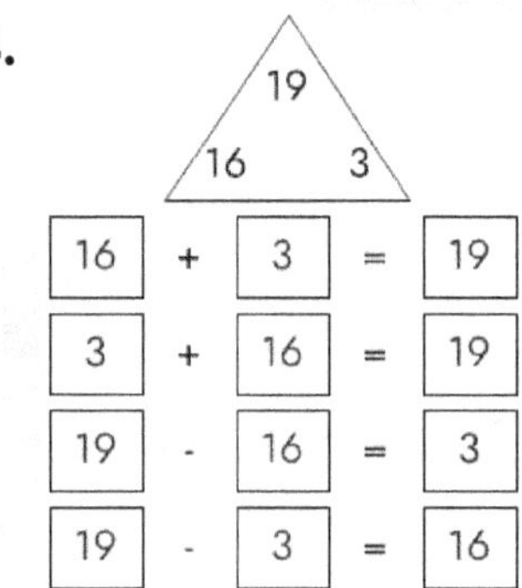

16	+	3	=	19
3	+	16	=	19
19	-	16	=	3
19	-	3	=	16

5.
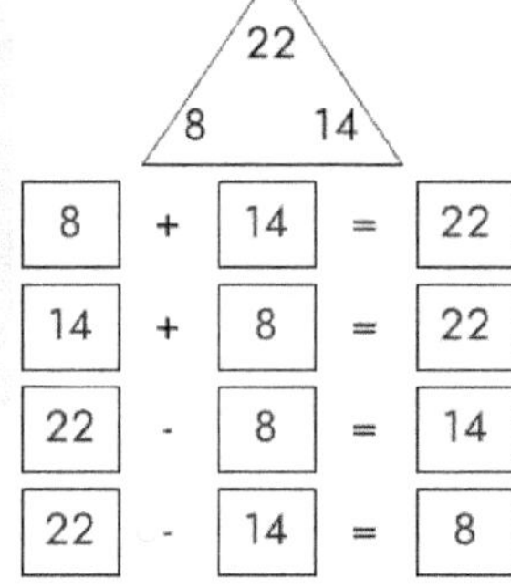

8	+	14	=	22
14	+	8	=	22
22	-	8	=	14
22	-	14	=	8

6.
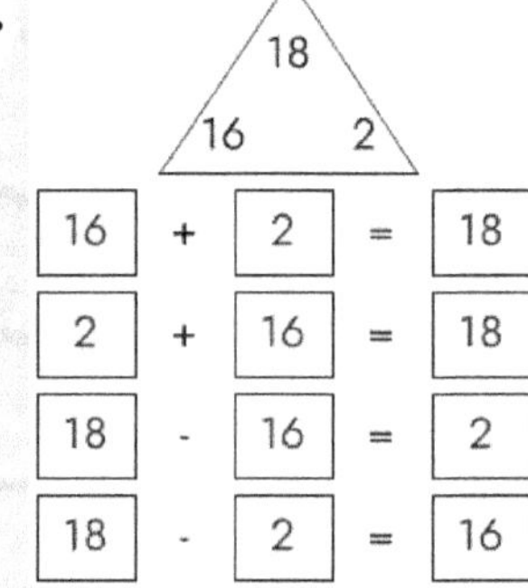

16	+	2	=	18
2	+	16	=	18
18	-	16	=	2
18	-	2	=	16

7.
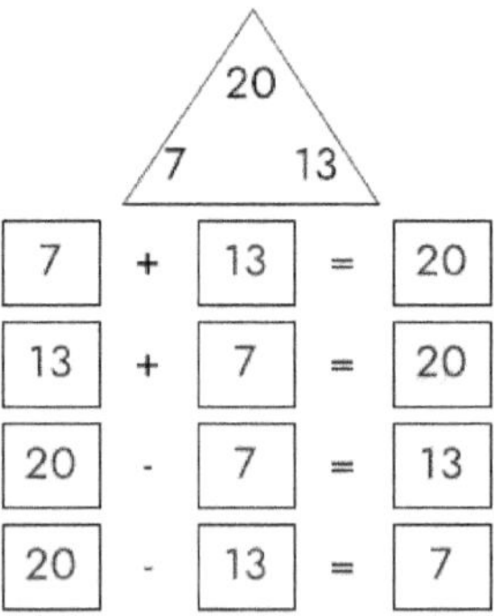

7	+	13	=	20
13	+	7	=	20
20	-	7	=	13
20	-	13	=	7

8.

12	+	2	=	14
2	+	12	=	14
14	-	12	=	2
14	-	2	=	12

9.

17	+	15	=	32
15	+	17	=	32
32	-	17	=	15
32	-	15	=	17

10. 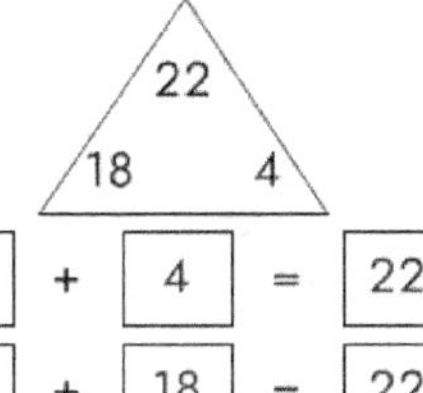

18	+	4	=	22
4	+	18	=	22
22	-	18	=	4
22	-	4	=	18

11. 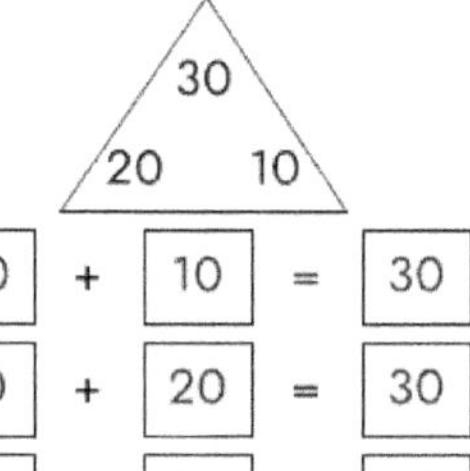

14	+	9	=	23
9	+	14	=	23
23	-	14	=	9
23	-	9	=	14

12.

20	+	10	=	30
10	+	20	=	30
30	-	20	=	10
30	-	10	=	20

13. 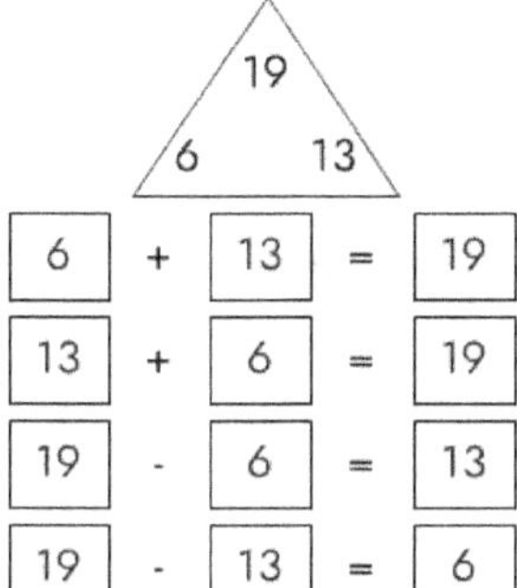

6	+	13	=	19
13	+	6	=	19
19	-	6	=	13
19	-	13	=	6

14. 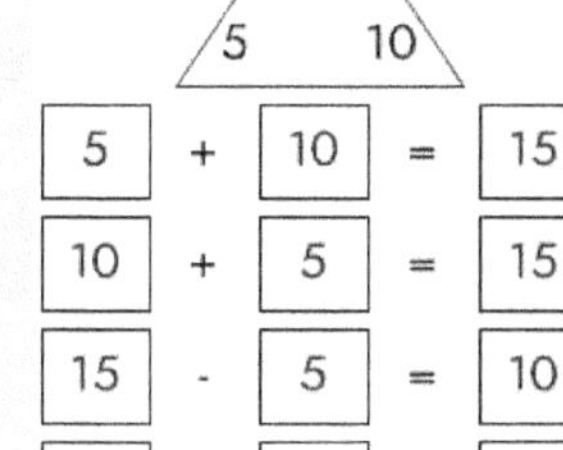

5	+	10	=	15
10	+	5	=	15
15	-	5	=	10
15	-	10	=	5

15. 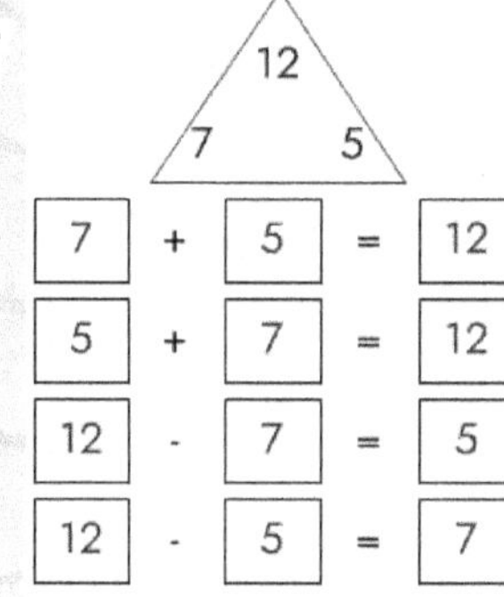

7	+	5	=	12
5	+	7	=	12
12	-	7	=	5
12	-	5	=	7

16. 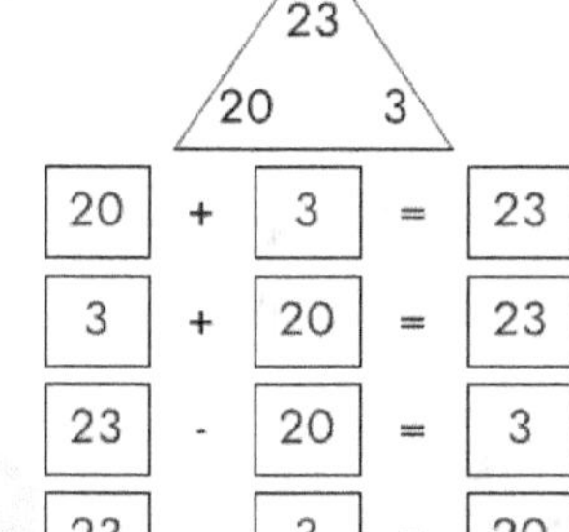

20	+	3	=	23
3	+	20	=	23
23	-	20	=	3
23	-	3	=	20

17. 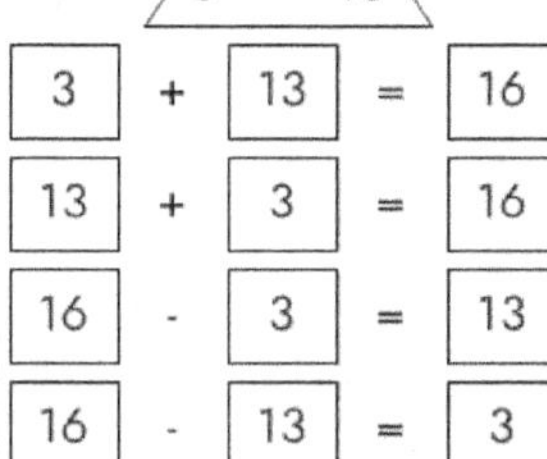

3	+	13	=	16
13	+	3	=	16
16	-	3	=	13
16	-	13	=	3

18.

11	+	15	=	26
15	+	11	=	26
26	-	11	=	15
26	-	15	=	11

19. 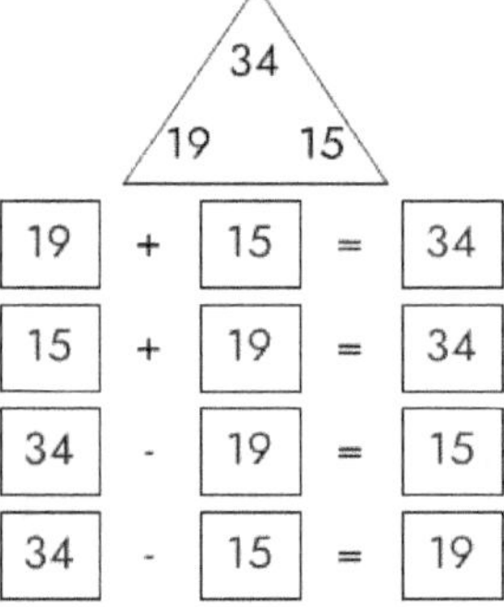

19	+	15	=	34
15	+	19	=	34
34	−	19	=	15
34	−	15	=	19

20. 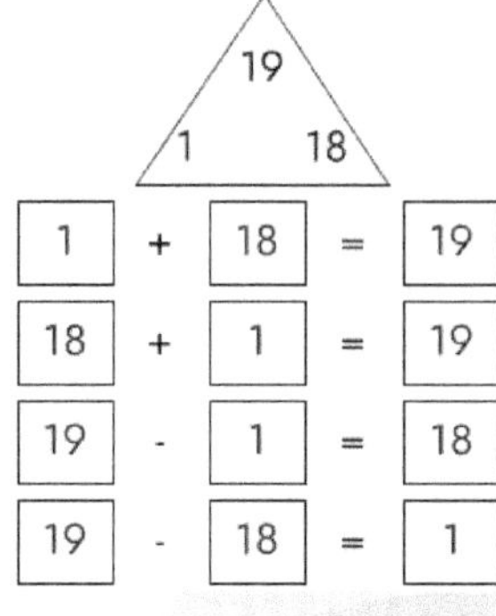

1	+	18	=	19
18	+	1	=	19
19	−	1	=	18
19	−	18	=	1

21. 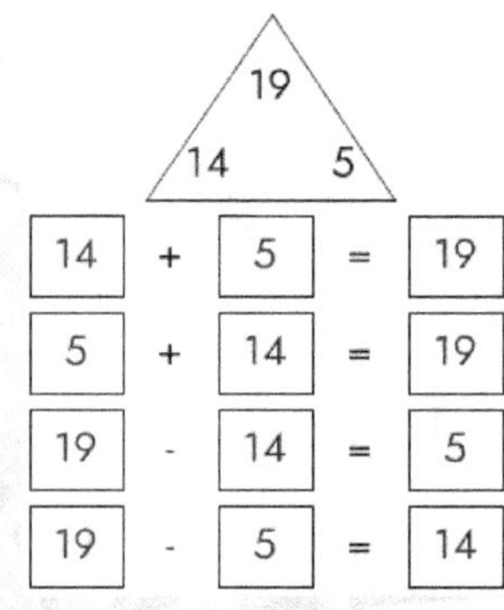

14	+	5	=	19
5	+	14	=	19
19	−	14	=	5
19	−	5	=	14

22. 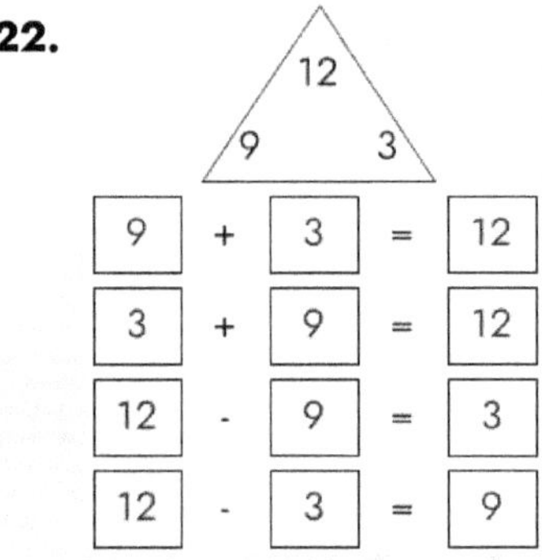

9	+	3	=	12
3	+	9	=	12
12	−	9	=	3
12	−	3	=	9

23. 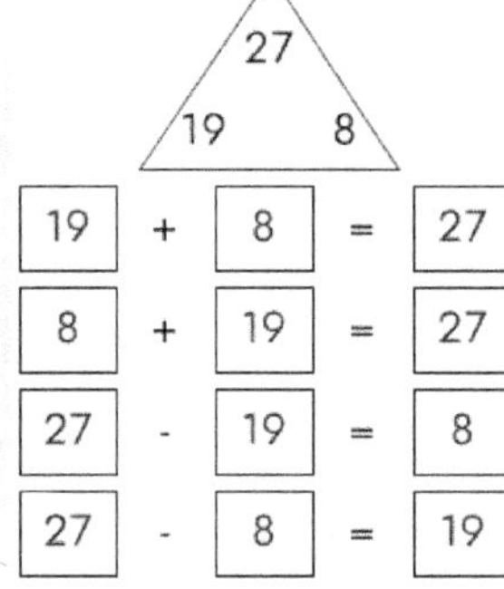

19	+	8	=	27
8	+	19	=	27
27	−	19	=	8
27	−	8	=	19

24. 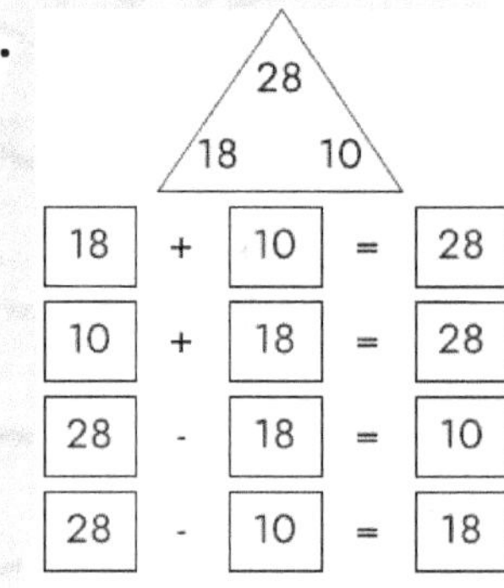

18	+	10	=	28
10	+	18	=	28
28	−	18	=	10
28	−	10	=	18

25. 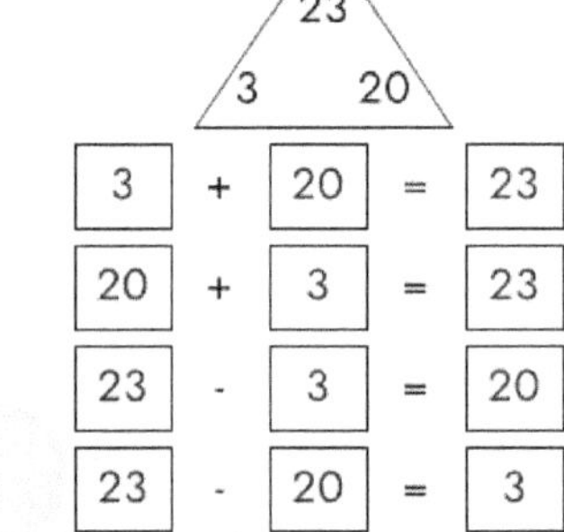

3	+	20	=	23
20	+	3	=	23
23	−	3	=	20
23	−	20	=	3

26. 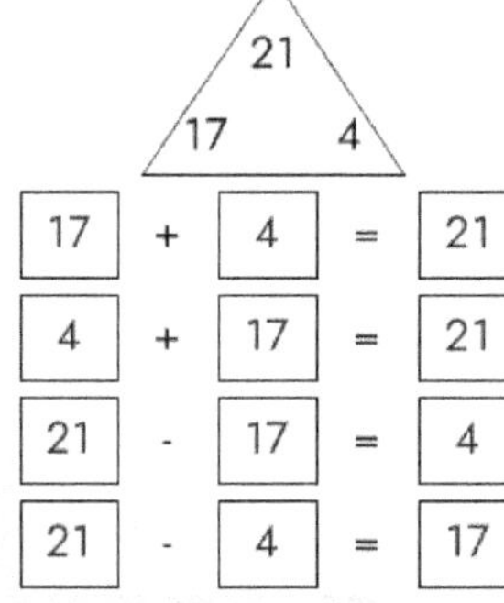

17	+	4	=	21
4	+	17	=	21
21	−	17	=	4
21	−	4	=	17

27. 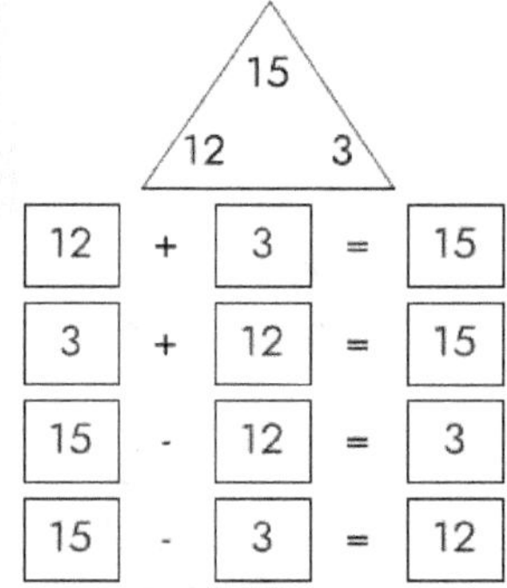

12	+	3	=	15
3	+	12	=	15
15	−	12	=	3
15	−	3	=	12

28.

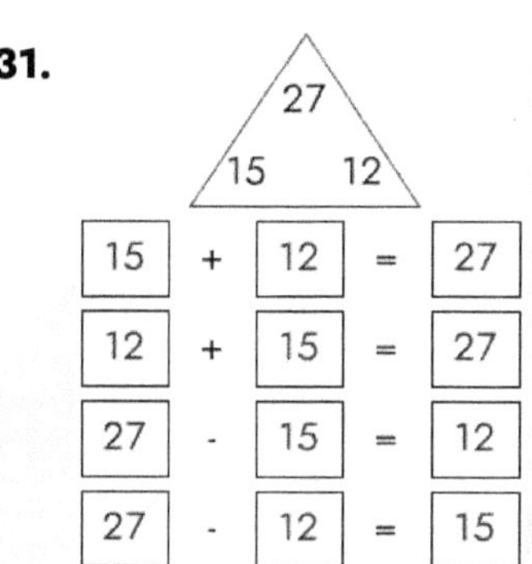

12	+	9	=	21
9	+	12	=	21
21	-	12	=	9
21	-	9	=	12

29.

14	+	15	=	29
15	+	14	=	29
29	-	14	=	15
29	-	15	=	14

30.

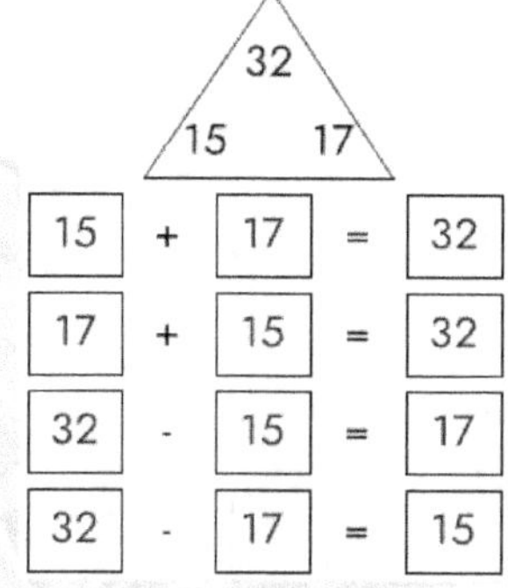

15	+	17	=	32
17	+	15	=	32
32	-	15	=	17
32	-	17	=	15

31.

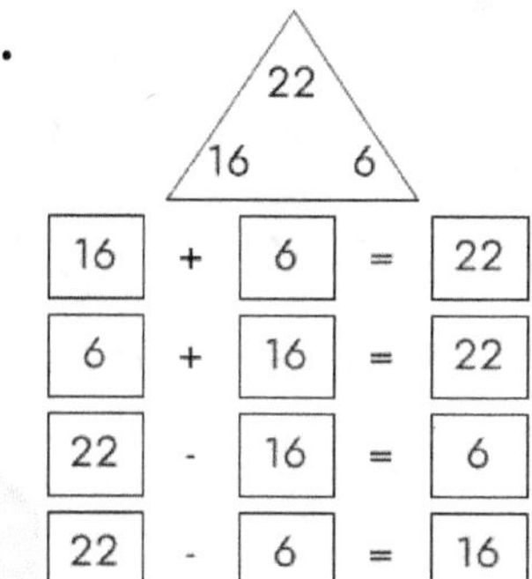

15	+	12	=	27
12	+	15	=	27
27	-	15	=	12
27	-	12	=	15

32.

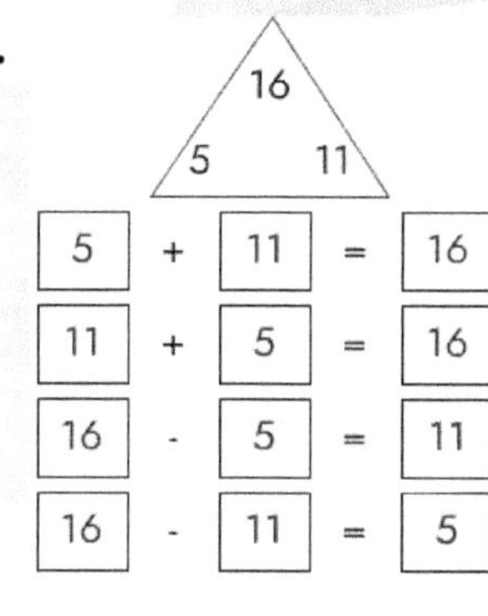

5	+	11	=	16
11	+	5	=	16
16	-	5	=	11
16	-	11	=	5

33.

3	+	16	=	19
16	+	3	=	19
19	-	3	=	16
19	-	16	=	3

34.

16	+	6	=	22
6	+	16	=	22
22	-	16	=	6
22	-	6	=	16

35.

4	+	14	=	18
14	+	4	=	18
18	-	4	=	14
18	-	14	=	4

36.

14	+	11	=	25
11	+	14	=	25
25	-	14	=	11
25	-	11	=	14

37.

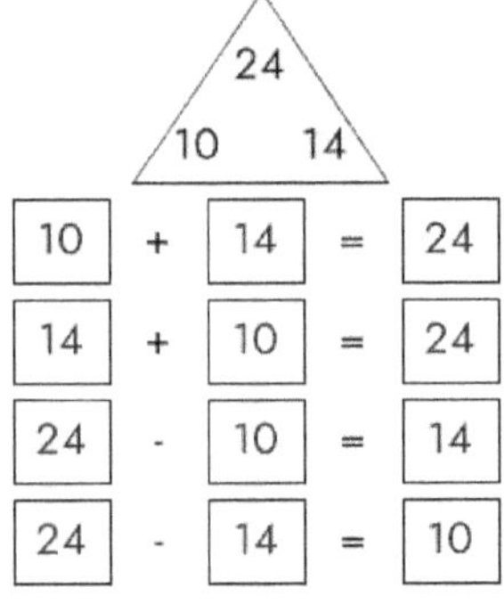

10	+ 14	= 24
14	+ 10	= 24
24	- 10	= 14
24	- 14	= 10

38.

1	+ 4	= 5
4	+ 1	= 5
5	- 1	= 4
5	- 4	= 1

39.

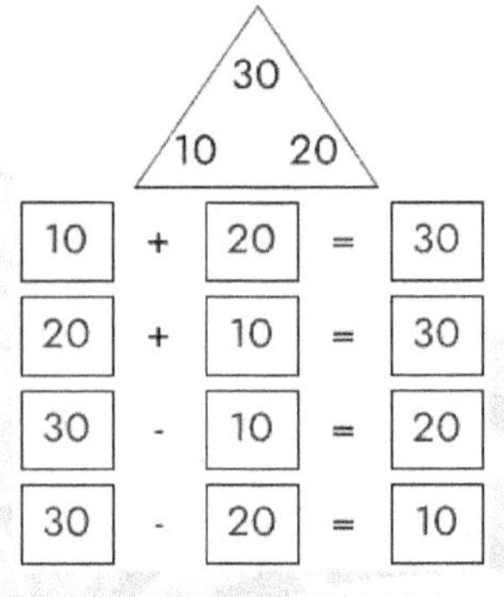

10	+ 20	= 30
20	+ 10	= 30
30	- 10	= 20
30	- 20	= 10

40.

20	+ 1	= 21
1	+ 20	= 21
21	- 20	= 1
21	- 1	= 20

Page 47: Mixed Two-Digit Practice

1. 27 **2.** 1 **3.** 54 **4.** 66 **5.** 3 **6.** 77 **7.** 75 **8.** 74 **9.** 68

10. 30 **11.** 38 **12.** 56 **13.** 20 **14.** 64 **15.** 30 **16.** 9 **17.** 59 **18.** 57

19. 5 **20.** 52 **21.** 64 **22.** 1 **23.** 14 **24.** 7 **25.** 77 **26.** 78 **27.** 14

28. 78 **29.** 52 **30.** 96 **31.** 36 **32.** 70 **33.** 0 **34.** 3 **35.** 23 **36.** 29

37. 44 **38.** 58 **39.** 38 **40.** 64 **41.** 47 **42.** 77 **43.** 42 **44.** 94 **45.** 88

46. 70 **47.** 65 **48.** 51 **49.** 24 **50.** 52 **51.** 40 **52.** 3 **53.** 47 **54.** 58

55. 3 **56.** 24 **57.** 54 **58.** 31 **59.** 47 **60.** 37 **61.** 33 **62.** 14 **63.** 40

64. 37 **65.** 5 **66.** 0 **67.** 82 **68.** 82 **69.** 80 **70.** 46 **71.** 12 **72.** 4

73. 97 **74.** 22 **75.** 3 **76.** 16

Page 51:   Addition with Regrouping

1. 110	**2.** 161	**3.** 133	**4.** 132	**5.** 130	**6.** 120	**7.** 181	**8.** 152
9. 156	**10.** 182	**11.** 140	**12.** 146	**13.** 126	**14.** 142	**15.** 113	**16.** 111
17. 120	**18.** 140	**19.** 130	**20.** 140	**21.** 110	**22.** 151	**23.** 140	**24.** 112
25. 111	**26.** 168	**27.** 112	**28.** 132	**29.** 136	**30.** 127	**31.** 120	**32.** 120
33. 133	**34.** 144	**35.** 110	**36.** 173	**37.** 143	**38.** 140	**39.** 116	**40.** 140
41. 142	**42.** 154	**43.** 120	**44.** 140	**45.** 170	**46.** 111	**47.** 120	**48.** 140
49. 140	**50.** 132	**51.** 160	**52.** 112	**53.** 120	**54.** 134	**55.** 150	**56.** 130
57. 126	**58.** 115	**59.** 123	**60.** 123	**61.** 124	**62.** 152	**63.** 120	**64.** 122
65. 110	**66.** 133	**67.** 155	**68.** 151	**69.** 110	**70.** 121	**71.** 114	**72.** 120
73. 112	**74.** 141	**75.** 163	**76.** 113				

Page 55:   Subtraction with Regrouping

1. 7	**2.** 42	**3.** 58	**4.** 5	**5.** 8	**6.** 19	**7.** 9	**8.** 45	**9.** 19
10. 8	**11.** 8	**12.** 28	**13.** 17	**14.** 35	**15.** 6	**16.** 52	**17.** 36	**18.** 36
19. 48	**20.** 8	**21.** 27	**22.** 3	**23.** 29	**24.** 29	**25.** 28	**26.** 9	**27.** 8
28. 27	**29.** 29	**30.** 18	**31.** 9	**32.** 79	**33.** 6	**34.** 9	**35.** 17	**36.** 19
37. 56	**38.** 19	**39.** 18	**40.** 15	**41.** 9	**42.** 6	**43.** 79	**44.** 8	**45.** 8
46. 26	**47.** 7	**48.** 6	**49.** 6	**50.** 39	**51.** 7	**52.** 29	**53.** 29	**54.** 26
55. 12	**56.** 29	**57.** 9	**58.** 8	**59.** 16	**60.** 29	**61.** 8	**62.** 9	**63.** 29
64. 17	**65.** 9	**66.** 6	**67.** 17	**68.** 45	**69.** 39	**70.** 8	**71.** 29	**72.** 14
73. 9	**74.** 17	**75.** 7	**76.** 3					

Page 59: Can you Make 100?

1. 64	**2.** 84	**3.** 96	**4.** 69	**5.** 82	**6.** 91	**7.** 79	**8.** 73	**9.** 63
10. 89	**11.** 95	**12.** 78	**13.** 66	**14.** 86	**15.** 71	**16.** 72	**17.** 90	**18.** 74
19. 94	**20.** 85	**21.** 92	**22.** 97	**23.** 65	**24.** 87	**25.** 77	**26.** 67	**27.** 83
28. 88	**29.** 93	**30.** 61	**31.** 70	**32.** 75	**33.** 76	**34.** 98	**35.** 99	**36.** 80

Page 61: Place Value

1. 3 tens	**2.** 7 tens	**3.** 3 ones	**4.** 9 tens
5. 3 tens	**6.** 9 ones	**7.** 3 hundreds	**8.** 4 tens
9. 5 hundreds	**10.** 0 tens	**11.** 8 tens	**12.** 1 hundred
13. 2 ones	**14.** 8 ones	**15.** 4 tens	**16.** 2 hundreds
17. 3 ones	**18.** 4 ones	**19.** 4 tens	**20.** 1 one
21. 7 tens	**22.** 8 hundreds	**23.** 1 ten	**24.** 8 hundreds
25. 3 hundreds	**26.** 2 hundreds	**27.** 1 ten	**28.** 3 ones
29. 4 ones	**30.** 9 ones	**31.** 1 ten	**32.** 7 tens
33. 6 hundreds	**34.** 4 tens	**35.** 7 tens	**36.** 8 tens
37. 2 ones	**38.** 5 hundreds	**39.** 1 one	**40.** 3 ones
41. 2 tens	**42.** 8 ones	**43.** 8 hundreds	**44.** 9 hundreds
45. 7 tens	**46.** 8 hundreds	**47.** 0 tens	**48.** 9 ones
49. 4 ones	**50.** 1 hundred	**51.** 8 hundreds	**52.** 5 ones
53. 2 tens	**54.** 7 hundreds	**55.** 1 hundred	**56.** 4 hundreds
57. 1 hundred	**58.** 5 ones	**59.** 7 hundreds	**60.** 9 hundreds
61. 1 ten	**62.** 5 hundreds	**63.** 1 ten	**64.** 2 tens

65. 1 hundred   **66.** 9 hundreds   **67.** 0 ones   **68.** 3 tens

69. 9 tens   **70.** 7 hundreds

Page 65:   Place Value: Expanded Notation

1. 348   **2.** 446   **3.** 21   **4.** 508   **5.** 298   **6.** 551   **7.** 975   **8.** 363

9. 648   **10.** 924   **11.** 613   **12.** 560   **13.** 803   **14.** 566   **15.** 641   **16.** 835

17. 62   **18.** 123   **19.** 144   **20.** 243   **21.** 503   **22.** 945   **23.** 980   **24.** 524

25. 477   **26.** 98   **27.** 205   **28.** 811   **29.** 158   **30.** 468   **31.** 423   **32.** 198

33. 469   **34.** 867   **35.** 804   **36.** 818   **37.** 714   **38.** 938   **39.** 883   **40.** 773

41. 242   **42.** 652   **43.** 80   **44.** 386   **45.** 569   **46.** 946   **47.** 514   **48.** 72

49. 771   **50.** 182   **51.** 950   **52.** 671   **53.** 320   **54.** 101   **55.** 570   **56.** 403

57. 466   **58.** 497   **59.** 31   **60.** 201   **61.** 165   **62.** 206   **63.** 181   **64.** 502

65. 415   **66.** 92   **67.** 935   **68.** 762   **69.** 823   **70.** 122   **71.** 124   **72.** 240

73. 371   **74.** 3   **75.** 851   **76.** 865   **77.** 595   **78.** 955   **79.** 532   **80.** 584

81. 133   **82.** 41   **83.** 976   **84.** 518   **85.** 752   **86.** 878   **87.** 369   **88.** 402

89. 353   **90.** 218   **91.** 907   **92.** 683   **93.** 426   **94.** 78   **95.** 447   **96.** 900

Page 73: Addition Quiz

1. 37	**7.** 38	**13.** 29	**19.** 5
2. 21	**8.** 33	**14.** 32	**20.** 29
3. 33	**9.** 20	**15.** 7	**21.** 32
4. 14	**10.** 24	**16.** 24	**22.** 26
5. 27	**11.** 15	**17.** 27	**23.** 11
6. 15	**12.** 34	**18.** 15	**24.** 18

Page 77: Subtraction Quiz

1. 10	**7.** 15	**13.** -10	**19.** 3
2. 1	**8.** -1	**14.** -1	**20.** 3
3. 8	**9.** 3	**15.** 6	**21.** 13
4. 3	**10.** -3	**16.** 14	**22.** 1
5. -1	**11.** -3	**17.** 6	**23.** 6
6. -2	**12.** -7	**18.** -1	**24.** 8

www.ingramcontent.com/pod-product-compliance
Lightning Source LLC
Chambersburg PA
CBHW080837160726
47999CB00009B/2924